More Praise for *The Argonauts*

"Maggie Nelson is one of the most electrifying writers at work in America today, among the sharpest and most supple thinkers of her generation. . . . *[The Argonauts]* is about love and marriage, motherhood, pregnancy, birth and family-making, and because it is a book by Maggie Nelson, it turns every one of these concepts on its head. . . . Generative and generous, this is a book that belongs on the shelves of anyone who desires, especially if what they desire is nothing short of freedom itself."   —*The Guardian*

"A book about using the writings of smart, even difficult writers to help us find clarity and precision in our intimate lives, and it's a book about the no less intimate pleasures of the life of the mind. . . . A magnificent achievement of thought, care and art."   —*Los Angeles Times*

"Maggie Nelson slays entrenched notions of gender, marriage, and sexuality with lyricism, intellectual brass, and soul-ringing honesty."   —*Vanity Fair*

"So much writing about motherhood makes the world seem smaller after the child arrives, more circumscribed, as if in tacit fealty to the larger cultural assumptions about moms and domesticity; Nelson's book does the opposite."
                    —*The New York Times Book Review*

"A lushly poetic intellectual oasis. . . . Nelson weaves straightforward personal history with deeply intelligent meditations on what it all means. . . . A courageous, heady, poetic and irresistible book."   —*San Francisco Chronicle*

"Nelson's hybrid book suggests a new path for the memoir. There's no need for falls from grace or stirring redemptions when you can look at life and death, as Nelson does, with a refined critical eye. It doesn't hurt that she speaks with the voice of a poet either."   —*Vulture*

"One of my favorite books of the last few years. . . . In some ways, this book is a life-changer in that it posits new spheres of both being and togetherness."
                    —Carrie Brownstein, *T Magazine*

"Nelson's vibrant, probing and, most of all, outstanding book is also a philosophical look at motherhood, transitioning, partnership, parenting, and family—an examination of the restrictive way we've approached these terms in the past and the ongoing struggle to arrive at more inclusive and expansive definitions for them."   —NPR

"I read *The Argonauts* in one breathless, tearful, mind-blown day and I'm still recovering."   —Miranda July, *Harper's Bazaar*

"The kind of book you feel desperate to share. . . . An important and impassioned book, one you will feel better for having read."   —*Salon*

"Astounding. . . . If I had to chose a book for everyone I know to read, it would be this one."   —*Bitch*

"Maggie Nelson explores the frontiers of thinking about love, language, and family, adding to a stunning body of work unconstrained by labels of form and genre."   —*Poets & Writers*

"At once a work in the tradition of surgical critics of self and art like Susan Sontag and in a category of writing entirely new. . . . If you want to think—or better yet, to imagine—in ways you never before thought possible, read this book."   —*Brooklyn Quarterly*

"This is a queer book in its softest heart, totally defiant and simultaneously full of love and a desire to connect with the world. This might all sound esoteric but the book is solid as a fucking rock: you'll devour it."
—*Electric Literature*

"*[The Argonauts]* contains multitudes. It's a love letter to her fluidly gendered partner, the artist Harry Dodge. It's an appreciation of her favorite queer thinkers. It's a chronicle of first-time motherhood. It's also the best kind of nonfiction read, the kind that enlarges one's reading list by half."
—*Lambda Literary*

"*The Argonauts* is deeply, personally and movingly about love. . . . A considered rejection of false choices, an intelligent, irritating, theoretical, intimate, funny, sad and exhilarating testament to the ever-fluid process of seeing out and getting out."   —*Star Tribune* (Minneapolis)

"Nelson proposes a completely different way of looking at sex and sexuality, child-rearing and childbirth and everything else." —*London Review of Books*

"Warm, winning, sprawling, inexhaustible." —*n+1*

"What makes this book such a pleasure to read is Nelson's fierce intellect, which she thrillingly aims at the body. . . . Maggie Nelson is one of the best writers alive." —*Full-Stop*

"The very act of reading *The Argonauts* feels revolutionary." —*Barnes & Noble Review*

"[Nelson] writes beautifully about the deeply sensory, even sensual, joy that her child brings her, and about the difficulty of disentangling this mother love from other loves. . . . In its constant motion between criticism and memoir, *The Argonauts* is a thrilling realization of that effort so central to so many queer and feminist lives: the effort to live (with) our theory." —*Feministing*

"Reading Nelson is like sweeping the leaves out of your mental driveway: by the end of one of her books, you have a better understanding of how the world works. . . . The result is one of the most intelligent, generous, and moving books of the year." —*Publishers Weekly*

"A fiercely provocative and intellectually audacious memoir. . . . The author turns the whole process and concept of motherhood inside out, exploring every possible perspective, blurring the distinctions among the political, philosophical, aesthetic and personal." —*Kirkus Reviews*, starred review

"Maggie Nelson cuts through our culture's prefabricated structures of thought and feeling with an intelligence whose ferocity is ultimately in the service of love. No piety is safe, no orthodoxy, no easy irony. The scare quotes burn off like fog." —Ben Lerner

"Once again, Maggie Nelson has created an awe-inspiring work, one that smartly calls bullshit on the places culture—radical subcultures included—stigmatize and misunderstand both maternity and queer family making. With a fiercely vulnerable intelligence, Nelson leaves no area un-investigated, including her own heart. I know of no other book like this, and I know how crucially the culture needs it." —Michelle Tea

"In the seventeenth century a book like Maggie Nelson's *The Argonauts* might have been called an anatomy, by which I mean it's a learned, quirky, open-hearted, often beautiful naming-of-parts. The anatomy never forgets the fragile embodied world—its carnality or its finitude. Merely by describing her works and days, Nelson—like a kind of female Voltaire—could be said to wage staunch battle against the as-yet-undead forces of banality, stupidity, prejudice, and moral sloth." —Terry Castle

"There isn't another critic alive like Maggie Nelson—who writes with such passion, clarity, explicitness, fluidity, playfulness, and generosity that she redefines what thinking can do today. Nelson soars through art and philosophy and her own experiences with reckless mastery and insurrectionary ease—a virtuosity born of deep reflection and fearless trust in what literature, at its best, can do." —Wayne Koestenbaum

"Maggie Nelson's *The Argonauts* makes the socialization of the maternal function—the dispersed, dispersive essence of the futurity we present to one another until one is not another anymore—palpable as feeling and thought. There's the violence we commit in making a claim for that futurity, and the violence we endure when that claim is denied; there's the love story buried in every 'I love you,' and in every 'I love you' there's a contract for destruction and rebuilding; there's *The Argonauts,* which is one of the greatest books I've ever read." —Fred Moten

"What a dazzlingly generous, gloriously unpredictable book! Maggie Nelson shows us what it means to be real, offering a way of thinking that is as challenging as it is liberating. She invites us to 'pay homage to the transitive' and enjoy 'a becoming in which one never becomes.' Reading *The Argonauts* made me happier and freer." —Eula Biss

"*The Argonauts* takes us on a delicious journey into the real life intimacies and intricacies of queer love, sex, literature, and motherhood. Maggie Nelson's honesty, intelligence, humor and great writing transform what society might deem a radical, nontraditional lifestyle into the new desirable. A fucking gem of a book that touched and tickled all my sweet spots." —Annie Sprinkle

"In *The Argonauts,* Maggie Nelson turns 'making the personal public' into a romantic, intellectual wet dream. A gorgeous book, inventive, fearless, and full of heart." —Kim Gordon

THE ARGONAUTS

ALSO BY MAGGIE NELSON

On Freedom: Four Songs of Care and Constraint
The Art of Cruelty: A Reckoning
Bluets
Women, the New York School, and Other True Abstractions
The Red Parts: Autobiography of a Trial
Jane: A Murder
Something Bright, Then Holes
The Latest Winter
Shiner

THE ARGONAUTS

Maggie Nelson

Graywolf Press

This publication is made possible, in part, by the voters of Minnesota through a Minnesota State Arts Board Operating Support grant, thanks to a legislative appropriation from the arts and cultural heritage fund, and through a grant from the Wells Fargo Foundation Minnesota. Significant support has also been provided by Target, the McKnight Foundation, the Amazon Literary Partnership, and other generous contributions from foundations, corporations, and individuals. To these organizations and individuals we offer our heartfelt thanks.

The Argonauts is a project of the Creative Capital Foundation.

Published by Graywolf Press
250 Third Avenue North, Suite 600
Minneapolis, Minnesota 55401

www.graywolfpress.org

Published in the United States of America

ISBN 978-1-55597-707-8 (cloth)
ISBN 978-1-55597-735-1 (paper)

14 16 18 20 21 19 17 15 13

Library of Congress Control Number: 2015953599

Cover design: Jeenee Lee Design

for Harry

THE ARGONAUTS

October, 2007. The Santa Ana winds are shredding the bark off the eucalyptus trees in long white stripes. A friend and I risk the widowmakers by having lunch outside, during which she suggests I tattoo the words HARD TO GET across my knuckles, as a reminder of this pose's possible fruits. Instead the words *I love you* come tumbling out of my mouth in an incantation the first time you fuck me in the ass, my face smashed against the cement floor of your dank and charming bachelor pad. You had *Molloy* by your bedside and a stack of cocks in a shadowy unused shower stall. Does it get any better? *What's your pleasure?* you asked, then stuck around for an answer.

Before we met, I had spent a lifetime devoted to Wittgenstein's idea that the inexpressible is contained—inexpressibly!—in the expressed. This idea gets less air time than his more reverential *Whereof one cannot speak thereof one must be silent,* but it is, I think, the deeper idea. Its paradox is, quite literally, *why I write,* or how I feel able to keep writing.

For it doesn't feed or exalt any angst one may feel about the incapacity to express, in words, that which eludes them. It doesn't punish what can be said for what, by definition, it cannot be. Nor does it ham it up by miming a constricted throat: *Lo, what I would say, were words good enough.* Words are good enough.

It is idle to fault a net for having holes, my encyclopedia notes.

In this way you can have your empty church with a dirt floor swept clean of dirt and your spectacular stained glass gleaming by the cathedral rafters, both. Because nothing you say can fuck up the space for God.

I've explained this elsewhere. But I'm trying to say something different now.

Before long I learned that you had spent a lifetime equally devoted to the conviction that words are *not* good enough. Not only not good enough, but corrosive to all that is good, all that is real, all that is flow. We argued and argued on this account, full of fever, not malice. Once we name something, you said, we can never see it the same way again. All that is unnameable falls away, gets lost, is murdered. You called this the cookie-cutter function of our minds. You said that you knew this not from shunning language but from immersion in it, on the screen, in conversation, onstage, on the page. I argued along the lines of Thomas Jefferson and the churches—for plethora, for kaleidoscopic shifting, for excess. I insisted that words did more than nominate. I read aloud to you the opening of *Philosophical Investigations. Slab,* I shouted, *slab!*

For a time, I thought I had won. You conceded there might be an OK human, an OK human animal, even if that human animal used language, even if its use of language were somehow defining of its humanness—even if humanness itself meant trashing and torching the whole motley, precious planet, along with its, our, future.

But I changed too. I looked anew at unnameable things, or at least things whose essence is flicker, flow. I readmitted the sadness of our eventual extinction, and the injustice of our extinction of others. I stopped smugly repeating *Everything that can be thought at all can be thought clearly* and wondered anew, can everything be thought.

Ludwig
Wittgenstein

And you—whatever you argued, you never mimed a constricted throat. In fact you ran at least a lap ahead of me, words streaming in your wake. How could I ever catch up (by which I mean, *how could you want me?*).

A day or two after my love pronouncement, now feral with vulnerability, I sent you the passage from *Roland Barthes by Roland Barthes* in which Barthes describes how the subject who utters the phrase "I love you" is like "the Argonaut renewing his ship during its voyage without changing its name." Just as the *Argo*'s parts may be replaced over time but the boat is still called the *Argo,* whenever the lover utters the phrase "I love you," its meaning must be renewed by each use, as "the very task of love and of language is to give to one and the same phrase inflections which will be forever new."

I thought the passage was romantic. You read it as a possible retraction. In retrospect, I guess it was both.

You've punctured my solitude, I told you. It had been a useful solitude, constructed, as it was, around a recent sobriety, long walks to and from the Y through the sordid, bougainvillea-strewn back streets of Hollywood, evening drives up and down Mulholland to kill the long nights, and, of course, maniacal bouts of writing, learning to address no one. But the time for its puncturing had come. *I feel I can give you everything without giving myself away,* I whispered in your basement bed. If one does one's solitude right, this is the prize.

A few months later, we spent Christmas together in a hotel in downtown San Francisco. I had booked the room for us online, in the hope that my booking of the room and our time in the room would make you love me forever. It turned out to be one of those hotels that booked for cheap because it was undergoing an astonishingly rude renovation, and because it was smack in the middle of the cracked-out Tenderloin. No matter—we had other business to attend to. Sun filtered through the ratty venetian blinds just barely obscuring the construction workers hammering away outside as we attended to it. *Just don't kill me,* I said as you took off your leather belt, smiling.

After the Barthes, I tried again, this time with a fragment of a poem by Michael Ondaatje:

Kissing the stomach
kissing your scarred
skin boat. History
is what you've travelled on
and take with you

We've each had our stomachs
kissed by strangers
to the other

and as for me
I bless everyone
who kissed you here

I didn't send the fragment because I had in any way achieved its serenity. I sent it with the aspiration that one day I might— that one day my jealousy might recede, and I would be able to behold the names and images of others inked onto your skin without disjunct or distaste. (Early on we made a romantic visit to Dr. Tattoff on Wilshire Boulevard, both of us giddy at the prospect of clearing your slate. We left crestfallen at the price, the improbability of ever completely eradicating the ink.)

After lunch, my friend who suggested the HARD TO GET tattoo invites me to her office, where she offers to Google you on my behalf. She's going to see if the Internet reveals a preferred pronoun for you, since despite or due to the fact that we're spending every free moment in bed together and already talking about moving in, I can't bring myself to ask. Instead I've become a quick study in pronoun avoidance. The key is training your ear not to mind hearing a person's name over and over again. You must learn to take cover in grammatical cul-de-sacs, relax into an orgy of specificity. You must learn to tolerate an instance beyond the Two, precisely at the moment of attempting to represent a partnership—a nuptial, even. *Nuptials are the opposite of a couple. There are no longer binary machines: question-answer, masculine-feminine, man-animal, etc. This could be what a conversation is—simply the outline of a becoming.*

Gilles Deleuze/
Claire Parnet

Expert as one may become at such a conversation, to this day it remains almost impossible for me to make an airline reservation or negotiate with my human resources department on our behalf without flashes of shame or befuddlement. It's not really my shame or befuddlement—it's more like I'm ashamed for (or simply pissed at) the person who keeps making all the wrong presumptions and has to be corrected, but who can't be corrected because the words are not good enough.

How can the words not be good enough?

Lovesick on the floor of my friend's office, I squint up at her as she scrolls through an onslaught of bright information I don't want to see. I want the you no one else can see, the you so close the third person never need apply. "Look, here's a quote from John Waters, saying, 'She's very handsome.' So maybe you should use 'she.' I mean, it's *John Waters*." *That was years ago,* I roll my eyes from the floor. *Things might have changed.*

When making your butch-buddy film, *By Hook or By Crook,* you and your cowriter, Silas Howard, decided that the butch characters would call each other "he" and "him," but in the outer world of grocery stores and authority figures, people would call them "she" and "her." The point wasn't that if the outer world were schooled appropriately re: the characters' preferred pronouns, everything would be right as rain. Because if the outsiders called the characters "he," it would be a different kind of he. Words change depending on who speaks them; there is no cure. The answer isn't just to introduce new words *(boi, cis-gendered, andro-fag)* and then set out to reify their meanings (though obviously there is power and pragmatism here). One must also become alert to the multitude of possible uses, possible contexts, the wings with which each word can fly. Like when you whisper, *You're just a hole, letting me fill you up.* Like when I say *husband.*

Soon after we got together, we attended a dinner party at which a (presumably straight, or at least straight-married) woman who'd known Harry for some time turned to me and said, "So, have you been with other women, before Harry?" I was taken aback. Undeterred, she went on: "Straight ladies have always been hot for Harry." Was Harry a woman? Was I a straight lady? What did past relationships I'd had with "other women" have in common with this one? Why did I have to think about other "straight ladies" who were hot for my Harry? Was his sexual power, which I already felt to be immense, a kind of spell I'd fallen under, from which I would emerge abandoned, as he moved on to seduce others? Why was this woman, whom I barely knew, talking to me like this? When would Harry come back from the bathroom?

There are people out there who get annoyed at the story that Djuna Barnes, rather than identify as a lesbian, preferred to say that she "just loved Thelma." Gertrude Stein reputedly made similar claims, albeit not in those exact terms, about Alice. I get why it's politically maddening, but I've also always thought it a little romantic—the romance of letting an individual experience of desire take precedence over a categorical one. The story brings to mind art historian T. J. Clark's defense of his interest in the eighteenth-century painter Nicolas Poussin from imaginary interlocutors: "Calling an interest in Poussin nostalgic or elitist is like calling the interest one has, say, in the person one cares for most deeply 'hetero- (or homo-) sexist,' or 'exclusive' or 'proprietorial.' Yes, that may be right: those may be roughly the parameters, and regrettable; but the interest itself may still be more complete and human—still carry more of human possibility and compassion—than interests uncontaminated by any such affect or compulsion." Here, as elsewhere, contamination *makes deep* rather than disqualifies.

Besides, everyone knows that Barnes and Stein had relationships with women besides Thelma and Alice. Alice knew, too: she was apparently so jealous upon finding out that Stein's early novel *Q. E. D.* told the coded story of a love triangle involving Stein and a certain May Bookstaver that Alice—who was also Stein's editor and typist—found all sorts of weasely ways to omit every appearance of the word *May* or *may* when she retyped Stein's *Stanzas in Meditation,* henceforth an unwitting collaboration.

By February I was driving around the city looking at apartment after apartment, trying to find one big enough for us and your son, whom I hadn't yet met. Eventually we found a house on a hill with gleaming dark wood floors and a view of a mountain and a too-high rent. The day we got the keys, we slept together in a fit of giddiness on a thin blanket spread out over the wood floor of what would become our first bedroom.

That view. It may have been a pile of rough scrub with a stagnant pond at its top, but for two years, it was our mountain.

And then, just like that, I was folding your son's laundry. He had just turned three. Such little socks! Such little underwear! I marveled at them, made him lukewarm cocoa each morning with as much powder as can fit in the rim of a fingernail, played Fallen Soldier with him for hours on end. In Fallen Soldier he would collapse with all his gear on—sequined chain mail hat, sword, sheath, a limb wounded from battle, tied up in a scarf. I was the good Blue Witch who had to sprinkle healing dust all over him to bring him back to life. I had a twin who was evil; the evil twin had felled him with her poisonous blue powder. But now I was here to heal him. He lay there motionless, eyes closed, the faintest smile on his face, while I recited my monologue: *But where could this soldier have come from? How did he get so far from home? Is he badly wounded? Will he be kind or fierce when he awakens? Will he know I am good, or will he mistake me for my evil twin? What can I say that will bring him back to life?*

Throughout that fall, yellow YES ON PROP 8 signs were sprouting up everywhere, most notably jabbed into an otherwise bald and beautiful mountain I passed each day on my way to work. The sign depicted four stick figures raising their hands to the sky, in a paroxysm of joy—the joy, I suppose, of heteronormativity, here indicated by the fact that one of the stick figures sported a triangle skirt. *(What is that triangle, anyway? My twat?)* PROTECT CALIFORNIA CHILDREN! the stick figures cheered.

Each time I passed the sign stuck into the blameless mountain, I thought about Catherine Opie's *Self-Portrait/Cutting* from 1993, in which Opie photographed her back with a drawing of a house and two stick-figure women holding hands (two triangle skirts!) carved into it, along with a sun, a cloud, and two birds. She took the photo while the drawing was still dripping with blood. "Opie, who had recently broken up with her partner, was longing at the time to start a family, and the image radiates all the painful contradictions inherent in that wish," *Art in America* explains.

I don't get it, I said to Harry. Who wants a version of the Prop 8 poster, but with two triangle skirts?

Maybe Cathy does, Harry shrugged.

Once I wrote a book about domesticity in the poetry of certain gay men (Ashbery, Schuyler) and some women (Mayer, Notley). I wrote this book when I was living in New York City in a teeny, too-hot attic apartment on a Brooklyn thoroughfare underlined by the F train. I had an unusable stove filled with petrified mouse droppings, an empty fridge save for a couple of beers and yogurt peanut honey Balance bars, a futon on a piece of plywood unevenly balanced on milk crates for a bed, and a floor through which I could hear *Standcleartheclosingdoors* morning, noon, and night. I spent approximately seven hours a day lying in bed in this apartment, if that. Mostly I slept elsewhere. I wrote most everything I wrote and read most everything I read in public, just as I am writing this in public now.

I was so happy renting in New York City for so long because renting—or at least the way I rented, which involved never lifting a finger to better my surroundings—allows you to let things literally fall apart all around you. Then, when it gets to be too much, you just move on.

Susan Fraiman Many feminists have argued for *the decline of the domestic as a separate, inherently female sphere and the vindication of domesticity as an ethic, an affect, an aesthetic, and a public.* I'm not sure what this vindication would mean, exactly, though I think in my book I was angling for something of the same. But even then I suspected that I was doing so because I didn't have a domestic, and I liked it that way.

I liked Fallen Soldier because it gave me time to learn about your son's face in mute repose: big almond eyes, skin just starting to freckle. And clearly he found some novel, relaxing pleasure in just lying there, protected by imaginary armor, while a near stranger who was quickly becoming family picked up each limb and turned it over, trying to find the wound.

Not long ago, a friend came over to our house and pulled down a mug for coffee, a mug that was a gift from my mother. It's one of those mugs you can purchase online from Snapfish, with the photo of your choice emblazoned on it. I was horrified when I received it, but it's the biggest mug we own, so we keep it around, in case someone's in the mood for a trough of warm milk or something.

Wow, my friend said, filling it up. *I've never seen anything so heteronormative in all my life.*

The photo on the mug depicts my family and me, all dressed up to go to the *Nutcracker* at Christmastime—a ritual that was important to my mother when I was a little girl, and that we have revived with her now that there are children in my life. In the photo I'm seven months pregnant with what will become Iggy, wearing a high ponytail and leopard print dress; Harry and his son are wearing matching dark suits, looking dashing. We're standing in front of the mantel at my mother's house, which has monogrammed stockings hanging from it. We look happy.

But what about it is the essence of heteronormativity? That my mother made a mug on a boojie service like Snapfish? That we're clearly participating, or acquiescing into participating, in a long tradition of families being photographed at holiday time in their holiday best? That my mother made me the mug, in part to indicate that she recognizes and accepts my tribe as family? What about my pregnancy—is that inherently heteronormative? Or is the presumed opposition of queerness and procreation (or, to put a finer edge on it, maternity) more a reactionary embrace of how things have shaken down for queers than the mark of some ontological truth? As more queers have kids, will the presumed opposition simply wither away? Will you miss it?

Is there something inherently queer about pregnancy itself, insofar as it profoundly alters one's "normal" state, and occasions a radical intimacy with—and radical alienation from—one's body? How can an experience so profoundly strange and wild and transformative also symbolize or enact the ultimate conformity? Or is this just another disqualification of anything tied too closely to the female animal from the privileged term (in this case, nonconformity, or radicality)? What about the fact that Harry is neither male nor female? *I'm a special—a two for one,* his character Valentine explains in *By Hook or By Crook.*

Judith Butler When or how do *new kinship systems mime older nuclear-family arrangements* and when or how do they *radically recontextualize them in a way that constitutes a rethinking of kinship*? How can you tell; or, rather, who's to tell? *Tell your girlfriend to find a different kid to play house with,* your ex would say, after we first moved in.

To align oneself with the real while intimating that others are at play, approximate, or in imitation can feel good. But any fixed claim on realness, especially when it is tied to an identity, also has a finger in psychosis. Jacques Lacan *If a man who thinks he is a king is mad, a king who thinks he is a king is no less so.*

Perhaps this is why psychologist D. W. Winnicott's notion of "feeling real" is so moving to me. One can aspire to feel real, one can help others to feel real, and one can oneself feel real—a feeling Winnicott describes as the collected, primary sensation of aliveness, "the aliveness of the body tissues and working of body-functions, including the heart's action and breathing," which makes spontaneous gesture possible. For Winnicott, feeling real is not reactive to external stimuli, nor is it an identity. It is a sensation—a sensation that spreads. Among other things, it makes one want to live.

Some people find pleasure in aligning themselves with an identity, as in *You make me feel like a natural woman*—made famous by Aretha Franklin and, later, by Judith Butler, who focused on the instability wrought by the simile. But there can also be a horror in doing so, not to mention an impossibility. *It's not possible to live twenty-four hours a day soaked in the immediate awareness of one's sex. Gendered selfconsciousness has, mercifully, a flickering nature.*

Denise Riley

A friend says he thinks of gender as a color. Gender does share with color a certain ontological indeterminacy: it isn't quite right to say that an object *is* a color, nor that the object *has* a color. Context also changes it: *all cats are gray,* etc. Nor is color *voluntary,* precisely. But none of these formulations means that the object in question is *colorless.*

The bad reading [of Gender Trouble*] goes something like this: I can get up in the morning, look in my closet, and decide which gender I want to be today. I can take out a piece of clothing and change my gender: stylize it, and then that evening I can change it again and be something radically other, so that what you get is something like the commodification of gender, and the understanding of taking on a gender as a kind of consumerism. . . . When my whole point was that the very formation of subjects, the very formation of persons,* presupposes *gender in a certain way—that gender is not to be chosen and that "performativity" is not radical choice and it's not voluntarism. . . . Performativity has to do with repetition, very often with the repetition of oppressive and painful gender norms to force them to resignify. This is not freedom, but a question of how to work the trap that one is inevitably in.*

Butler

You should order a mug in response, my friend mused while drinking her coffee. *Like, how about one that features Iggy's head crowning, in all its bloody glory?* (I had told her earlier that day that I was vaguely hurt that my mother hadn't wanted to look at my birth photos; Harry then reminded me that few people ever want to look at anyone's birth photos, at least not the graphic ones. And I was forced to admit that my past feelings about other people's birth photos bore out the truth of this statement. But in my postpartum haze, I felt as though giving birth to Iggy was such an achievement, and doesn't my mother like to be proud of my achievements? She *laminated* the page in the *New York Times* that listed me as a Guggenheim recipient, for God's sake. Unable to throw the Guggenheim placemat away (ingratitude), but not knowing what else to do with it, I've since placed it below Iggy's high chair, to catch the food that flows downward. Given that the fellowship essentially paid for his conception, each time I sponge tidbits of shredded wheat or broccoli florets off of it, I feel a loose sense of justice.)

During our first forays out as a couple, I blushed a lot, felt dizzy with my luck, unable to contain the nearly exploding fact that I've so obviously gotten everything I'd ever wanted, everything there was to get. *Handsome, brilliant, quick-witted, articulate, forceful, you.* We spent hours and hours on the red couch, giggling, *The happiness police are going to come and arrest us if we go on this way. Arrest us for our luck.*

Deborah Hay   *What if where I am is what I need?* Before you, I had always thought of this mantra as a means of making peace with a bummer or even catastrophic situation. I never imagined it might apply to joy, too.

In *The Cancer Journals,* Audre Lorde rails against the imperative to optimism and happiness that she found in the medical discourse surrounding breast cancer. "Was I really fighting the spread of radiation, racism, woman-slaughter, chemical invasion of our food, pollution of our environment, the abuse and psychic destruction of our young, merely to avoid dealing with my first and greatest responsibility—to be happy?" Lorde writes. "Let us seek 'joy' rather than real food and clean air and a saner future on a liveable earth! As if happiness alone can protect us from the results of profit-madness."

Happiness is no protection, and certainly it is not a responsibility. *The freedom to be happy restricts human freedom if you are not free to be not happy.* But one can make of either freedom a habit, and only you know which you've chosen.

Sara Ahmed

The wedding story of Mary and George Oppen is one of the only straight-people stories I know in which the marriage is made more romantic by virtue of its being a sham. Here is their story: One night in 1926, Mary went out on a date with George, whom she knew just a little from a college poetry class. As Mary remembers it: "He came for me in his roommate's Model T Ford, and we drove out to the country, sat and talked, made love, and talked until morning. . . . We talked as we had never talked before, an outpouring." Upon returning to their dorms in the morning, Mary found herself expelled; George was suspended. They then took off together, hitchhiking on the open road.

Before meeting George, Mary had decided firmly against marriage, considering it to be a "disastrous trap." But she also knew that traveling together without being married put her and George at risk with the law, via the Mann Act—one of the many laws in U.S. history ostensibly passed to prosecute unequivocally bad things like sexual slavery, but which in actuality has been used to harass anyone whose relationships the state deems "immoral."

So in 1927, Mary got married. Here is her account of that day:

> Although I had a strong conviction that my relationship with George was not an affair of the State, the threat of imprisonment on the road frightened us, so we went to be married in Dallas. A girl we met gave me her purple velvet dress, her boyfriend gave us a pint of gin. George wore his college roommate's baggy plus-fours, but we did not drink the gin. We bought a ten-cent ring and went to the ugly red sandstone courthouse that still stands in Dallas. We gave my name, Mary Colby, and the name George was using, "David Verdi," because he was fleeing from his father.

And so Mary Colby marries David Verdi, but she never precisely marries George Oppen. They give the state the slip, along with George's wealthy family (who by this point had hired a private eye to find them). That slip then becomes a sliver of light filtering into their house for the next fifty-seven years. Fifty-seven years of baffling the paradigm, with ardor.

I have long known about madmen and kings; I have long known about feeling real. I have long been lucky enough to *feel* real, no matter what diminishments or depressions have come my way. And I have long known that the *moment of queer pride is a refusal to be shamed by witnessing the other as being ashamed of you.*

So why did your ex's digs about playing house sting so bright?

Sometimes one has to know something many times over. Sometimes one forgets, and then remembers. And then forgets, and then remembers. And then forgets again.

As with knowledge, so too, with presence.

If the baby could speak to the mother, says Winnicott, here is what it might say:

> I find you;
> You survive what I do to you as I come to recognize you as
>   not-me;
> I use you;
> I forget you;
> But you remember me;
> I keep forgetting you;
> I lose you;
> I am sad.

Winnicott's concept of "good enough" mothering is in resurgence right now. You can find it everywhere from mommy blogs to Alison Bechdel's graphic novel *Are You My Mother?* to reams of critical theory. (One of this book's titles, in an alternate universe: *Why Winnicott Now?*)

Despite his popularity, however, you still can't procure an intimidating multivolume set titled *The Collected Works of D. W. Winnicott.* His work has to be encountered in little bits—bits that have been contaminated by their relationship to actual, blathering mothers, or by otherwise middlebrow venues, which prohibit any easy enshrinement of Winnicott as a psychological heavyweight. In the back of one collection, I note the following sources for the essays therein: a presentation to the Nursery School Association of Great Britain and Northern Ireland; BBC broadcasts to mothers; a Q&A for a BBC program titled *Woman's Hour;* conferences about breast-feeding; lectures given to midwives; and "letters to the editor."

Such humble, contaminated sources are surely part of the reason why, in Iggy's first year of life, Winnicott was the only child psychologist who retained any interest or relevance for me. Klein's morbid infant sadism and bad breast, Freud's blockbuster Oedipal saga and freighted *fort/da,* Lacan's heavy-handed Imaginary and Symbolic—suddenly none seemed irreverent enough to address the situation of being a baby, of caretaking a baby. *Do castration and the Phallus tell us the deep Truths of Western culture or just the truth of how things are and might not always be?* It astonishes and shames me to think that I spent years finding such questions not only comprehensible, but compelling.

Elizabeth Weed

In the face of such phallocentric gravitas, I find myself drifting into a delinquent, anti-interpretive mood. *In place of a hermeneutics we need an erotics of art.* But even an erotics feels too heavy. I don't want an eros, or a hermeneutics, of my baby. Neither is dirty, neither is mirthful, enough.

Susan Sontag

On one of the long afternoons that has since bled into the one long afternoon of Iggy's infancy, I watch him pause on all fours at the threshold to our backyard, as he contemplates which scraggly oak leaf to scrunch toward first with his dogged army crawl. His soft little tongue, always whitened in the center from milk, nudges out of his mouth in gentle anticipation, a turtle bobbing out of its shell. I want to pause here, maybe forever, and hail the brief moment before I have to jump into action, before I must become the one who eliminates the *inappropriate object,* or, if I'm too late, who must harvest it from his mouth.

You, reader, are alive today, reading this, because someone once adequately policed your mouth exploring. In the face of this fact, Winnicott holds the relatively unsentimental position that we don't owe these people (often women, but by no means always) anything. But we do owe *ourselves* "an intellectual recognition of the fact that at first we were (psychologically) absolutely dependent, and that absolutely means absolutely. Luckily we were met by ordinary devotion."

By ordinary devotion, Winnicott means ordinary devotion. "It is a trite remark when I say that by devoted I simply mean devoted." Winnicott is a writer for whom ordinary words are good enough.

As soon as we moved in together, we were faced with the urgent task of setting up a home for your son that would feel abundant and containing—good enough—rather than broken or falling. (These poeticisms come from that classic of genderqueer kinship, *Mom's House, Dad's House.*) But that's not quite right—we knew about this task beforehand; it was, in fact, one of the reasons we moved so quickly. What became apparent was the urgent task specifically before me: that of learning how to be a stepparent. Talk about a potentially fraught identity! My stepfather had his faults, but every word I have ever uttered against him has come back to haunt me, now that I understand what it is to hold the position, to be held by it.

When you are a stepparent, no matter how wonderful you are, no matter how much love you have to give, no matter how mature or wise or successful or smart or responsible you are, you are structurally vulnerable to being hated or resented, and there is precious little you can do about it, save endure, and commit to planting seeds of sanity and good spirit in the face of whatever shitstorms may come your way. And don't expect to get any kudos from the culture, either: parents are Hallmark-sacrosanct, but stepparents are interlopers, self-servers, poachers, pollutants, and child molesters.

Every time I see the word *stepchild* in an obituary, as in "X is survived by three children and two stepchildren," or whenever an adult acquaintance says something like, "Oh, sorry, I can't make it—I'm visiting my stepdad this weekend," or when, during the Olympics, the camera pans the audience and the voiceover says, "there's X's stepmother, cheering him on," my heart skips a beat, just to hear the sound of the bond made public, made positive.

When I try to discover what I resent my stepfather for most, it is never "he gave me too much love." No—I resent him for not reliably giving the impression that he was glad he lived with my sister and me (he may not have been), for not telling me often that he loved me (again, he may not have—as one of the stepparenting self-help books I ordered during our early days put it, love is preferred, but not required), for not being my father, and for leaving after over twenty years of marriage to our mother without saying a proper good-bye.

I think you overestimate the maturity of adults, he wrote me in his final letter, a letter he sent only after I'd broken down and written him first, after a year of silence.

Angry and hurt as I may have been by his departure, his observation was undeniably correct. This slice of truth, offered in the final hour, ended up beginning a new chapter of my adulthood, the one in which I realized that age doesn't necessarily bring anything with it, save itself. The rest is optional.

Bear Family: my stepson's other favorite toddler game, which took place in our morning bed. In this game he was Baby Bear, a little bear with a speech impediment that forced him to say B's at every turn (Cousin Evan is Bousin Bevan, and so on).

Sometimes Baby Bear played at home with his bear family, delighting in his recalcitrant mispronunciations; other times he ventured off on his own, to spear a tuna. On one of these mornings, Baby Bear christened me *Bombi*—a relative of Mommy, but with a difference. I admired Baby Bear's inventiveness, which persists.

We hadn't been planning on getting married per se. But when we woke up on the morning of November 3, 2008, and listened to the radio's day-before-the-election polling as we made our hot drinks, it suddenly seemed as though Prop 8 was going to pass. We were surprised at our shock, as it revealed a passive, naive trust that the arc of the moral universe, however long, tends toward justice. But really justice has no coordinates, no teleology. We Googled "how to get married in Los Angeles" and set out for Norwalk City Hall, where the oracle promised the deed could be done, dropping our small charge off at day care on our way.

As we approached Norwalk—*where the hell are we?*—we passed several churches with variations of "one man + one woman: how God wants it" on their marquees. We also passed dozens of suburban houses with YES ON PROP 8 signs hammered into their lawns, stick figures indefatigably rejoicing.

Poor marriage! Off we went to kill it (unforgivable). Or reinforce it (unforgivable).

At Norwalk City Hall there were a bunch of white tents set up outside and a fleet of blue Eyewitness News vans idling in the lot. We started getting cold feet—neither of us was in the mood to become a poster child for queers marrying in hostile territory just prior to Prop 8's passage. We didn't want to show up in tomorrow's paper next to a frothing lunatic in cargo shorts waving a GOD HATES FAGS sign. Inside there was an epic line at the marriage counter, mostly fags and dykes of all ages, along with a slew of young straight couples, mostly Latino, who seemed bewildered by the nature of the day's crowd. The older men in front of us told us they got married a few months ago, but when their marriage certificate arrived in the mail, they noticed the signatures had been botched by their officiant. They were now desperately hoping for a re-do, so that they could stay officially married no matter what happened at the polls.

Contrary to what the Internet had promised, the chapel was all booked up, so all the couples in line were going to have to go elsewhere to get an official ceremony of some kind after finishing their paperwork. We struggled to understand how a contract with the so-called secular state could mandate some kind of spiritual ritual. People who already had officiants lined up to marry them later that day offered to make their ceremonies communal, to accommodate everyone who wanted to get married before midnight. The guys in front of us invited us to join their beach wedding in Malibu. We thanked them, but instead called 411 and asked for the name of a wedding chapel in West Hollywood—isn't that where the queers are? *I have a Hollywood Chapel on Santa Monica Boulevard,* the voice said.

The Hollywood Chapel turned out to be a hole in the wall at the end of the block where I lived for the loneliest three years of my life. Tacky maroon velvet curtains divided the waiting room from the chapel room; both spaces were decorated with cheap gothic candelabras, fake flowers, and a peach faux finish. A drag queen at the door did triple duty as a greeter, bouncer, and witness.

Reader, we married there, with the assistance of Reverend Lorelei Starbuck. Reverend Starbuck suggested we discuss the vows with her beforehand; we said they didn't really matter. She insisted. We let them stay standard, albeit stripped of pronouns. The ceremony was rushed, but as we said our vows, we were undone. We wept, besotted with our luck, then gratefully accepted two heart-shaped lollipops with THE HOLLYWOOD CHAPEL embossed on their wrappers, rushed to pick up the little guy at day care before closing, came home and ate chocolate pudding all together in sleeping bags on the porch, looking out over our mountain.

That evening, Reverend Starbuck—who listed her denomination as "Metaphysical" on our forms—rush-delivered our paperwork, along with that of hundreds of others, to whatever authorities had been authorized to deem our speech act felicitous. By the end of the day, 52 percent of California voters had voted to pass Prop 8, thus halting "same-sex" marriages across the state, reversing the conditions of our felicity. The Hollywood Chapel disappeared as quickly as it had sprung up, waiting, perhaps, to emerge another day.

One of the most annoying things about hearing the refrain "same-sex marriage" over and over again is that I don't know many—if any—queers who think of their desire's main feature as being "same-sex." It's true that a lot of lesbian sex writing from the '70s was about being turned on, and even politically transformed, by an encounter with sameness. This encounter was, is, can be, important, as it has to do with seeing reflected that which has been reviled, with exchanging alienation or internalized revulsion for desire and care. To devote yourself to someone else's pussy can be a means of devoting yourself to your own. But whatever sameness I've noted in my relationships with women is not the sameness of Woman, and certainly not the sameness of parts. Rather, it is the shared, crushing understanding of what it means to live in a patriarchy.

My stepson is too old for Fallen Soldier or Bear Family now. As I write, he's listening to Funky Cold Medina on his iPod—eyes closed, in his gigantic body, lying on the red couch. Nine years old.

There's something truly strange about living in a historical moment in which the conservative anxiety and despair about queers bringing down civilization and its institutions (marriage, most notably) is met by the anxiety and despair so many queers feel about the failure or incapacity of queerness to bring down civilization and its institutions, and their frustration with the assimilationist, unthinkingly neoliberal bent of the mainstream GLBTQ+ movement, which has spent fine coin begging entrance into two historically repressive structures: marriage and the military. "I'm not the kind of faggot who wants to put a rainbow sticker on a machine gun," declares poet CAConrad. If there's one thing homonormativity reveals, it's the troubling fact that *you can be victimized and in no way be radical; it happens very often among homosexuals as with every other oppressed minority.*

Leo Bersani

This is not a devaluation of queerness. It is a reminder: if we want to do more than claw our way into repressive structures, we have our work cut out for us.

At the 2012 Pride intervention in Oakland, some antiassimilationist activists unfurled a banner that read: CAPITALISM IS FUCKING THE QUEER OUT OF US. A distributed pamphlet read:

> What is destructive to straight society—we know can never be commodified and purged of rebellion. So we maintain our stance—as fierce fags, queers, dykes and trans girls and bois and gender queers and all the combination and in be tweens and those that negate it all at the same time.

We bid[e] our time, striking here and there and fantasize
of a world where all of the exploited of the world can come
together and attack. We want to find you, comrade, if this
too is what you want.

For the total destruction of Capital,
bad bitches who will fuck your shit up.

I was glad for their intervention: there is some evil shit in this
world that needs fucking up, and the time for blithely asserting that sleeping with whomever you want however you want
is going to jam its machinery is long past. But I've never been
able to answer to *comrade,* nor share in this fantasy of attack. In
fact I have come to understand revolutionary language as a sort
of fetish—in which case, one response to the above might be,
Our diagnosis is similar, but our perversities are not compatible.

Perhaps it's the word *radical* that needs rethinking. But what
could we angle ourselves toward instead, or in addition? Open-
ness? Is that good enough, strong enough? You're *the only one*   Pema Chödrön
who knows when you're using things to protect yourself and keep
your ego together and when you're opening and letting things fall
apart, letting the world come as it is—working with it rather than
struggling against it. You're the only one who knows. And the
thing is, even you don't always know.

In October of 2012, when Iggy was about eight months old, I
was invited to speak at Biola University, an evangelical Christian
school near Los Angeles. Their art department's annual sym-
posium was to be dedicated to the topic of art and violence.
For a few weeks I wrestled with the invitation. It was a short
drive away; in one afternoon of work, I could pay for a month
of babysitting for Iggy. But then there was the outrageous fact
that the college expels students for being gay or engaging in

homosexual acts. (As with the U.S. military's Don't Ask, Don't Tell policy, Biola doesn't get bogged down with the question of whether homosexuality is an identity, a speech act, or a behavior: any which way, you're out.)

To learn more, I consulted Biola's doctrinal statement online, and there discovered that Biola actually disallows *all* sex outside of "biblical marriage," here defined as "a faithful, heterosexual union between one genetic male and one genetic female." (I was impressed by the "genetic"—très au courant!) Elsewhere on the web I learned that there is, or was, a student group called the Biola Queer Underground that emerged a few years ago to protest the antigay policies of the college, mainly via the web and anonymous postering campaigns on campus. The group's name seemed promising, but my excitement dimmed upon reading the FAQ on their web page:

> Q: What is The Biola Underground's stance on homosexuality?
>
> A: Surprisingly, some people have been unclear as to what we think about being both LGBTQ and Christian. To clear up this issue, we are in favor of celebrating homosexual behavior in its proper context: marriage. . . . We hold to the already stated standards of Biola that premarital sex is sinful and outside of God's plan for humans and we believe that this standard also applies to homosexuals and other members of the LGBTQ community.

What kind of "queer" is this?

Eve Kosofsky Sedgwick wanted to make way for "queer" to hold all kinds of resistances and fracturings and mismatches that have little or nothing to do with sexual orientation. "Queer is a continuing moment, movement, motive—recurrent, eddying, *troublant*," she wrote. "Keenly, it is relational, and strange." She wanted the term to be a perpetual excitement, a kind of placeholder—a nominative, like *Argo*, willing to designate molten or shifting parts, a means of asserting while also giving the slip. That is what reclaimed terms do—they retain, they insist on retaining, a sense of the fugitive.

At the same time, Sedgwick argued that "given the historical and contemporary force of the prohibitions against *every* same-sex sexual expression, for anyone to disavow those meanings, or to displace them from the term [*queer*]'s definitional center, would be to dematerialize any possibility of queerness itself."

In other words, she wanted it both ways. There is much to be learned from wanting something both ways.

Sedgwick once proposed that "what it takes—all it takes—to make the description 'queer' a true one is the impulsion *to* use it in the first person," and that "anyone's use of 'queer' about themselves means differently from their use of it about someone else." Annoying as it might be to hear a straight white guy talk about a book of his as queer (do you have to own everything?), in the end, it's probably all for the better. Sedgwick, who was long married to a man with whom she had, by her own description, mostly postshower, vanilla sex, knew about the possibilities of this first-person use of the term perhaps better than anyone else. She took heat for it, just as she took heat for identifying with gay men (not to mention *as* a gay man), and for giving lesbians not much more than an occasional nod. Some thought it regressive that a "queen of queer theory" kept men or male sexuality at the center of the action (as in her book

Between Men: English Literature and Male Homosocial Desire), even if for the purpose of feminist critique.

Such were Sedgwick's identifications and interests; she was nothing if not honest. And in person she exuded a sexuality and charisma that was much more powerful, particular, and compelling than the poles of masculinity and femininity could ever allow—one that had to do with being fat, freckled, prone to blushing, bedecked in textiles, generous, uncannily sweet, almost sadistically intelligent, and, by the time I met her, terminally ill.

The more I thought about Biola's doctrinal statement, the more I realized that I support private, consensual groups of adults deciding to live together however they please. If this particular cluster of adults doesn't want to have sex outside of "biblical marriage," then whatever. In the end, it was *this* sentence that kept me up at night: "Inadequate origin models [of the universe] hold that (a) God never directly intervened in creating nature and/or (b) humans share a common physical ancestry with earlier life forms." Our shared ancestry with earlier life forms is sacred to me. I declined the invitation. They booked a "story guru" from Hollywood in my place.

Flush with joy in our house on the hill, we were startled by some deep shadows. Your mother, whom I'd met but once, was diagnosed with breast cancer. Your son's custody remained unsettled, and the specter of a homophobic or transphobic judge deciding his fate, our family's fate, turned our days tornado green. You knocked yourself out to make him feel happy and held, set up a slide for him in our concrete sliver of a backyard, a baby pool in the front, a Lego station by the wall heater, a swing hanging from the studs in his bedroom. We read books all together before bed, then I would leave to give you two some alone time, listen to your soft voice singing "I've Been Working on the Railroad" night after night from behind the closed door. I read in one of my stepparenting guides that one should take stock of the developing bonds in a new family not every day or every month or every year, but every seven years. (Such a time frame struck me then as ludicrous; now, seven years later, as wise and luminous.) Your inability to live in your skin was reaching its peak, your neck and back pulsing with pain all day, all night, from your torso (and hence, your lungs) having been constricted for almost thirty years. You tried to stay wrapped even while sleeping, but by morning the floor was always littered with doctored sports bras, strips of dirty fabric— "smashers," you called them.

I just want you to feel free, I said in anger disguised as compassion, compassion disguised as anger.

Don't you get it yet? you yelled back. *I will never feel as free as you do, I will never feel as at home in the world, I will never feel as at home in my own skin. That's just the way it is, and always will be.*

Well then I feel really sorry for you, I said.

Or maybe, *Fine, but don't take me down with you.*

We knew something, maybe everything, was about to give. We hoped it wouldn't be us.

You showed me an essay about butches and femmes that contained the line "to be femme is to give honor where there has been shame." You were trying to tell me something, give me information I might need. I don't think that line is where you meant for me to stick—you may not even have noticed it—but there I stuck. I wanted and still want to give you any life-sustaining gift I have to offer; I beheld and still behold in anger and agony the eagerness of the world to throw piles of shit on those of us who want to savage or simply cannot help but savage the norms that so desperately need savaging. But I also felt mixed up: I had never conceived of myself as femme; I knew I had a habit of giving too much; I was frightened by the word *honor*. How could I tell you all that and stay inside our bubble, giggling on the red couch?

I told you I wanted to live in a world in which the antidote to shame is not honor, but honesty. You said I misunderstood what you meant by honor. We haven't yet stopped trying to explain to each other what these words mean to us; perhaps we never will.

You've written about all parts of your life except this, except the queer part, you said.

Give me a break, I said back. *I haven't written about it <u>yet.</u>*

In the midst of all this, we started to talk about getting pregnant. Whenever anyone asked me why I wanted to have a baby, I had no answer. But the muteness of the desire stood in inverse proportion to its size. I had felt the desire before, but in recent years I had given it up, or rather, I had given it over. And now here we were. Wanting, as so many want, the time to be right. But I was older now and less patient; I could already see that *give it over* would need to turn into *go get it,* and soon. When and how would we attempt it, how much mourning would there be if we turned away, what if we called and no baby spirit came.

As concepts such as "good enough" mothering suggest, Winnicott is a fairly sanguine soul. But he also takes pains to remind us what a baby will experience should the holding environment *not* be good enough:

The primitive agonies

Falling for ever
All kinds of disintegration
Things that disunite the psyche and the body

The fruits of privation

going to pieces
falling for ever
dying and dying and dying
losing all vestige of hope of the renewal of contacts

One could argue that Winnicott is speaking metaphorically here—as Michael Snediker has said in a more adult context: "One doesn't *really* shatter when one is fucked, despite Bersani's accounts of it as such." But while a baby may not die when its holding environment fails, it may indeed die and die and die. The question of what a psyche or a soul can experience depends, in large part, on what you believe it's made of. *Spirit is matter reduced to an extreme thinness: O so thin!*

Ralph Waldo
Emerson

In any case, Winnicott notably describes "the primitive agonies" not as lacks or voids, but as substantives: "fruits."

In 1984, George Oppen died of pneumonia with complications from Alzheimer's. Mary Oppen died a few years later, in 1990, of ovarian cancer. After George's death, several fragments of writing were found pinned to the wall above his desk. One of these read:

> Being with Mary: it has
> been almost too wonderful
> it is hard to believe

During our hard season, I thought a lot about this fragment. At times it filled me with an almost sadistic urge to unearth some kind of evidence that George and Mary had been unhappy, even if at moments—some sign that his writing might have ever come between them, that they didn't understand each other in some profound way, that they had ever exchanged ugly words, or differed on major decisions, such as whether George should fight in World War II, the efficacy of the Communist Party, whether to stay in exile in Mexico, and so on.

This wasn't schadenfreude. It was hope. I hoped that such things might have happened, and that Oppen, bobbing in the waves of bewilderment and lucidity that characterize a cruel neurological decline, would still be moved to write:

> Being with Mary: it has
> been almost too wonderful
> it is hard to believe

And so, shamefully, I looked. I looked for evidence of their unhappiness, all the while repressing the fact that my search reminded me of a particularly dysfunctional moment in Leonard Michaels's account of his tortured, explosive, and eventually disastrous relationship to his first wife, Sylvia. Upon learning that a friend had an equally horrible relationship with equally horrible fights, Michaels writes: "I was grateful to him, relieved, giddy with pleasure. So others lived this way, too. . . . Every couple, every marriage, was sick. Such thinking, like bloodletting, purged me. I was miserably normal; I was normally miserable." He and Sylvia marry; a short, miserable time later, she's dead from forty-seven Seconals.

Of course the Oppens fought and hurt each other sometimes, you said when I told you about my search. *They probably just kept it to themselves, out of respect and love for one another.*

Whatever I was looking for between George and Mary Oppen, I never found it. I did, however, find something I wasn't expecting. I found it in Mary's autobiography, *Meaning a Life,* which she published at the start of George's mental decline. I found Mary.

When I looked up *Meaning a Life* on Amazon, there was only one review. It was by a guy who gave the book a single star, complaining: "Purchased this book hoping to gain insight into the life of one of my favorite poets. Very little about George and a lot about Mary." *It's her autobiography, you fucking moron,* I thought, before realizing my trajectory had followed something of the same course.

Before the birth of her daughter, Linda, it turns out Mary suffered several stillbirths—too many, apparently, for her to give a number—as well as the crib death of a six-week-old. About all this, Mary writes:

Birth . . . I think I am afraid to try to write of it. In child-birth I was isolated; I never talked about it even to George. He was surprised to learn that giving birth was a peak emotional experience and so entirely my own that I never tried to express it. . . . I would wish it to remain whole, and I have preserved the wholeness of my own experience of birth by not telling it; it is too precious to me. Even now, writing of the experiences of age twenty-four to thirty, I wish to encompass my isolation and the wracking devas-tation of loss, the sense of being a nothing on the delivery table, knocked out by anesthetic, only to regain conscious-ness and be told once more, "The fetus is dead."

George and Mary are famous for living a life in conversation, in poetry. *We talked as I had never talked before, an outpouring.* But here, Mary is unsure that words are good enough. *I never talked about it even to George.* Her experience may be one of devastation, but she still worries that words might chip away at it (intolerable).

Nonetheless, years later, as her husband begins to peel away from language, Mary tries to tell.

In his epic treatise *Bubbles,* philosopher Peter Sloterdijk puts forth something he calls the "rule of a negative gynecology." To truly understand the fetal and perinatal world, Sloterdijk writes, "one must reject the temptation to extricate oneself from the affair with outside views of the mother-child relation-ship; where the concern is insight into intimate connections, outside observation is already the fundamental mistake." I ap-plaud this involution, this "cave research," this turn away from mastery and toward the immersive bubble of "blood, amniotic fluid, voice, sonic bubble and breath." I feel no urge to extricate myself from this bubble. But here's the catch: *I cannot hold my baby at the same time as I write.*

Winnicott acknowledges that the demands of ordinary devotion can be frightening for some mothers, who worry that giving themselves over to it will "turn them into a vegetable." Poet Alice Notley raises the stakes: "he is born and I am undone—feel as if I will / never be, was never born. // Two years later I obliterate myself again / having another child . . . for two years, there's no me here."

I have never felt that way, but I'm an old mom. I had nearly four decades to become myself before experimenting with my obliteration.

D. W. Winnicott

Sometimes mothers find it alarming to think that what they are doing is so important and in that case it is better not to tell them. It makes them self-conscious and then they do everything less well. . . . When a mother has a capacity quite simply to be a mother we must never interfere. She will not be able to fight for her rights because she will not understand.

As if mothers thought they were performing their ordinary devotions in the wild, then are stunned to look up, and see a peanut-crunching crowd across a moat.

Shortly after returning to work after having Iggy, I ran into a superior in the cafeteria. He gallantly purchased me my "vegan comfort meal" and a Naked juice. He asked when my next book would be out; I told him it might take a minute, as I had just had a baby. This sparked a story for him about a colleague he'd once had, a Renaissance studies professor, who allegedly found her newborn so fascinating that for two whole years, her Renaissance research struck her as esoteric and boring. *But then, after two years, her interest came back,* he said. *It came back,* he repeated, with a wink.

Over time, I have come to suspect that my affection for *Bubbles* may have less to do with its endorsement of the rule of negative gynecology, and more to do with its ridiculous title, which it shares with Michael Jackson's pet chimpanzee.

Michael doted on Bubbles. But Michael would also rotate the chimp out of service as it aged, and replace it with a new, younger Bubbles. (Cruelty of the *Argo?*)

When I was growing up, my mother would sometimes tell me to switch the TV channel to a station with a male weatherman. *They usually have the more accurate forecast,* she'd say.

The weather people are reading a script, I would say, rolling my eyes. *It's all the same forecast.*

It's just a feeling, she would shrug.

Alas, it isn't just a feeling. Even if women are consulting the same satellites, or reading from the same script: their reports are suspect; the jig is up. *In other words, the articulation of the reality of my sex is impossible in discourse, and for a structural, eidetic reason. My sex is removed, at least as the property of a subject, from the predicative mechanism that assures discursive coherence.*

Luce Irigaray

38

Irigaray's answer to this conundrum?: *to destroy . . . [but] with nuptial tools. . . . The option left to me,* she writes, *was to <u>have a fling with the philosophers.</u>*

In October of 1998, just a few weeks into my graduate school career, I was invited to attend a seminar with Jane Gallop and Rosalind Krauss. Gallop would be presenting new work, to which Krauss would respond. I was excited—back in college I had liked Gallop's heady, disobedient books on Lacan (such as *The Daughter's Seduction*); they evidenced a deep investment in Lacanian thought without seeming to have drunk the Kool-Aid. She was having a fling with the philosophers all right, but she seemed to be learning everything there was to know about the boiler room so that she could blow it up. Krauss's work I knew less well, but I gathered that everyone was invested in her theories about the modernist grid, and I liked the plain matte cover of *October* magazine. Didn't she write on Claude Cahun? I liked Claude Cahun. And busting the avant-garde's mythos of itself was, even then, my idea of a good time.

The professors gathered solemnly around a long wooden table in one of the more handsome rooms at the Grace Building, where CUNY was then situated. I felt as though I had truly arrived—somehow I had been plucked from the corner booth of Max Fish and deposited in the center of an intellectual mecca, complete with dark wood and academic superstars.

Gallop gave a slide show: her recent work was about being photographed by her husband, appropriately named Dick. I remember a photo of her with their baby boy in the bathtub, and one of her and her son lounging around together naked, Carole King–style. I remember being surprised and pleased that she was showing us naked photos of her and her son, and talking unabashedly about her partner Dick (heterosexuality always embarrasses me). She was trying to talk about photography from the standpoint of the photographed subject, which, as she said, "may be the position from which it is most difficult to claim valid general insights." And she was coupling this subjective position with that of being a mother, in an attempt to get at the experience of being photographed as a mother (another position generally assumed to be, as Gallop put it, "troublingly personal, anecdotal, self-concerned"). She was taking on Barthes's *Camera Lucida,* and the way in which even in Barthes—delectable Barthes!—the mother remains the (photographed) object; the son, the (writing) subject. "The writer is someone who plays with his mother's body," Barthes wrote. But sometimes the writer is also the mother (Möbius strip).

I liked that Gallop was onto something and letting us in on it before she fully understood it. She was hanging her shit out to dry: a start. She was droopy-eyed and louche in a way that I liked, and had that bad but endearing style that so many academics have—kind of stuck in the '80s, feather earrings, and so on. She even talked about how much she liked a shirt she was wearing in one of the slides—a black button-down with white bubbly scribbles all over it. I find it irresistibly interesting when people are cathected onto their bad style rather than simply oblivious to it (a description that may apply to us all; I sense the risk increases with age).

The slides were over, the talk was over, it was Krauss's turn. She scooted her chair up to the table and shuffled her papers. She was Gallop's inverse—sharp face, classy in a silk scarf, Ivy League, Upper East Side way. Feline, groomed, her thin dark hair in a bob. Kind of like the Janet Malcolm of art history. She started by saying how important Gallop's daring and thorough work on Lacan had been. This praise went on for some time.

Then, theatrically, she swerved. *The importance of this early work is why it is so deeply disturbing to behold the mediocrity, naïveté, and soft-mindedness of the work Gallop has presented to us today.* The color drained out of Gallop's face. Krauss ignored her, and went in for the kill.

The room thickened with the sound of one keenly intelligent woman taking another down. Dismembering her, really. Krauss excoriated Gallop for taking her own personal situation as subject matter, accused her of having an almost willful blindness to photography's long history. She alleged—or so I recall her alleging—that Gallop had misused Barthes, had failed to place her investigation in relation to any lineage of family photography, had punted on the most basic aesthetic concepts in art history, and so on. But the tacit undercurrent of her argument, as I felt it, was that Gallop's maternity had rotted her mind—besotted it with the narcissism that makes one think that an utterly ordinary experience shared by countless others is somehow unique, or uniquely interesting.

It's true that Gallop is no art historian, certainly not in the way that Krauss is. (Nor was Barthes, for that matter, but artistry trumps mastery.) And Krauss has always been something of a pugilist, just as Gallop has always been something of a narcissist—two perversities that proved, on this occasion, to be incompatible. But the lashing Gallop received that day stood for some time in my mind as an object lesson. Krauss acted as though Gallop should be ashamed for trotting out naked pictures of herself and her son in the bathtub, contaminating serious academic space with her pudgy body and unresolved, self-involved thinking (even though Gallop had been perfecting such contamination for years). But staging a fling with a philosopher was one thing; a pudgy mother in love with her son and her ugly scribble shirt was another.

I didn't have a baby then, nor did I have any designs on having one. Nor have I ever been what you might call a baby person (nor an animal person, nor a garden person, not even a house-plant person; even urgings toward "self-care" often irritate or mystify me). But I was enough of a feminist to refuse any knee-jerk quarantining of the feminine or the maternal from the realm of intellectual profundity. And, as I remember it, Krauss was not simply quarantining; she was shaming. In the face of such shaming, I felt no choice. I stood with Gallop.

In Arabic, the word for fetus derives from *jinn*, which means "hidden from sight." No matter how many ultrasounds you've had, no matter how well you feel you've gotten to know your baby's rhythms in utero, the baby's body is still a revelation. A body! An actual body! I was so in awe of Iggy's fantastic little body that it took a few weeks for me to feel that I had the right to touch him all over. Before Iggy, it always startled me to see a parent stuffing a Kleenex in the face of an unsuspecting toddler, as if a kid were just an object whose physical auton-omy could be violated any time some stray mucus appeared. I wanted to attend to Iggy, but I didn't want to *ambush* him. Also, the culture's worrying over pedophilia in all the wrong places at times made me feel unable to approach his genitals or anus with wonder and glee, until one day I realized, he's my baby, I can—indeed I must!—handle him freely and ably. My baby! My little butt! Now I delight in his little butt. I delight in pouring water over his head with a toy boat full of holes, wet-ting his blond curls, matted with butter from a plate he recently made into a hat.

Luckily, Iggy couldn't care less. He is stalwart, has a high toler-ance for physical intrusions. Within his first year of life, he with-stood a spinal tap, several catheterizations, a contrast enema, electric shocks, nuclear scans, countless IVs, and an infusion of rare antibodies harvested from other people's bodies (an infusion that, had we not had health insurance, would have cost $47,000 for the vial, an amount that puts the price of frozen sperm to shame). All that said, his native joy and robustness have continued, unabated. Until he grows too heavy, I carry him always and everywhere, even against the rules (making pancakes at the stove, walking down steep trails, etc.). When we go on the road together, I let him drag around my enormous rolly-bag at the airport, even though he's been ambulatory for only a few weeks. He insists. I recognize his insistence. I ignore the books that sternly advise against rocking or nursing your baby to sleep, so that she learns to go to sleep by herself; I am blessed with the time and the desire to hold Iggy until he slips off, and so I do. I wait and wait and wait until I hear a sleep rattle enter his breath, I watch his eyes flutter open and closed, open and closed, a hundred times, until finally they stay shut. I know from raising my stepson that this ritual won't last forever—Iggy's babyhood is already speeding away. By the time this book is published, it will be gone. Sturdy pilot, he flips over the coffee table and rides.

I adore Winnicott. But the perversity is not lost on me that the most oft-cited, well-respected, best-selling books about the caretaking of babies—Winnicott, Spock, Sears, Weissbluth—have been and are mostly still by men. On the front cover of *The Baby Book*—arguably one of the more progressive contemporary options (albeit oppressively heteronormative)—the byline reads "by William Sears (MD) and Martha Sears (RN)." This seems promising(ish), but nurse/wife/mother Martha's voice appears only in anecdotes, italics, and sidebars, never as co-narrator. Was she too busy taking care of their eight children to join in the first-person? I look down at my well-loved copy of *Winnicott on the Child* and note that it comes laden with not one, not two, but three introductions by male pediatricians (Brazelton, Greenspan, Spock). What kind of bubble would burst if a lady shrink were presumed to add value to his legacy? Why don't I myself seek out child-care books by women? Am I unconsciously channel-surfing for the male weatherman? How could Gallop, or any mother, however whip-smart, present the rule of negative gynecology and be taken as seriously as Sloterdijk? I'm boring myself with these reversals (feminist hazard).

In Dr. Sears's *The Baby Book* there's a little sidebar (written by Martha?) called "Sexual Feelings While Breastfeeding," which attempts to reassure you that such feelings don't mean you're a pedophile freak. It says that you're basically hormonal soup, and because the hormones unleashed by breast-feeding are the same as those unleashed by sex, you could be forgiven for the mix-up.

But how can it be a mix-up, if it's the same hormones? How does one go about partitioning one sexual feeling off from another, presumably more "real" sexual feeling? Or, more to the point, why the partition? It isn't *like* a love affair. It *is* a love affair.

Or, rather, it is romantic, erotic, and consuming—but without tentacles. I have my baby, and my baby has me. It is a buoyant eros, an eros without teleology. Even if I do feel turned on while I'm breast-feeding or rocking him to sleep, I don't feel the need to do anything about it (and if I did, it wouldn't be with him).

In the years to come, this affair will likely become unrequited, or so I've heard. All the more reason to hail the moment's autotelia.

It's so dark, this underspace, dark and sweaty. His thin hair is damp, smells like candy and earth, I burrow my mouth into it and breathe. I don't ever want to make the mistake of needing him as much as or more than he needs me. But there's no denying that sometimes, when we sleep together in the dark cavern of the bottom bunk, his big brother thrashing around on top, the white noise machine grinding out its fake rain, the green digital clock announcing every hour, Iggy's small body holds mine.

One of the most lovable aspects of Winnicott's writing on children (and on those who attempt to hold them) is his deployment of an "ordinary language" seemingly incapable of histrionics even as it discusses issues of maximum complexity and gravity. In his book *Queer Optimism,* Michael Snediker offers Winnicott's "nonironic denomination of adolescent depression as 'doldrums'" as an example of Winnicott's signature deflation-without-dismissal. "Easy enough . . . to wax lyrical on melancholy," Snediker writes, in reference to queer theory's long-standing preoccupation with melancholia. "Less easy to wax lyrical about 'doldrums.'"

One problem with lyrical waxing, as Snediker has it, is that it often signals (or occasions) an infatuation with overarching concepts or figures that can run roughshod over the specificities of the situation at hand. (Winnicott once accused Freud, for example, of using the concept of the death drive to "achieve a theoretical simplification that might be compared to the gradual elimination of detail in the technique of a sculptor like Michelangelo.")

Such accusations would not come as a surprise to many writers, especially to those who have attempted to pay homage, in their writing, to a beloved. Wayne Koestenbaum tells an instructive story on this account: "Some psycho girlfriend of mine (decades ago!) answered a long rhapsodic letter I'd written her with this terse, humiliating rebuff: 'Next time, write to me.' That one command, on a tiny slip of paper, tucked into an envelope. I remember thinking, 'Wasn't I writing to her? How could I know, when writing to her, that I secretly wasn't writing to her?' At that point, Derrida hadn't yet written *The Post Card,* so I didn't know what to do with my befuddled, wounded sense of being a rhapsodic narcissist of a letter-writer weirdly instructed to 'relate,' to speak to someone instead of to the nothingness at the end of writing."

The inexpressible may be contained (inexpressibly!) in the expressed, but the older I get, the more fearful I become of this nothingness, this waxing lyrical about those I love the most (Cordelia).

I finish a first draft of this book and give it to Harry. He doesn't have to tell me that he's read it: when I come home from work, I can see the pile of ruffled pages sticking out of his knapsack, and I can feel his mood, which one might describe as quiet ire. We agree to go out for lunch the next day to talk about it. At lunch he tells me he feels unbeheld—unheld, even. I know this is a terrible feeling. We go through the draft page by page, mechanical pencils in hand, with him suggesting ways I might facet my representation of him, of us. I try to listen, try to focus on his generosity in letting me write about him at all. He is, after all, a very private person, who has told me more than once that being with me is like an epileptic with a pacemaker being married to a strobe light artist. But nothing can substantively quell my inner defense attorney. *How can a book be both a free expression and a negotiation? Is it not idle to fault a net for having holes?*

That's just an excuse for a crappy net, he might say. *But it's my book, mine!* Yes, but the details of my life, of our life together, don't belong to you alone. *OK, but no mind can take the same interest in his neighbor's me as in his own. The neighbor's me falls together with all the rest of the things in one foreign mass, against which his own me stands out in startling relief.* A writer's narcissism. *But that's William James's description of subjectivity itself, not narcissism.* Whatever—why can't you just write something that will bear adequate witness to me, to us, to our happiness? *Because I do not yet understand the relationship between writing and happiness, or writing and holding.*

We used to talk about writing a book together; it was to be titled *Proximity.* Its ethos would derive from *Dialogues II,* co-authored by Gilles Deleuze and Claire Parnet: "As we became less sure what came from one, what came from the other, or even from someone else, we would become clearer about 'What is it to write?'"

Eventually, however, I realized that just the idea of such a merging was causing me too much anxiety. I guess I wasn't ready to lose sight of *my own me* yet, as for so long, writing has been the only place I have felt it plausible to find it (whatever "it" is).

Shame-spot: being someone who spoke freely, copiously, and passionately in high school, then arriving in college and realizing I was in danger of becoming one of those people who makes everyone else roll their eyes: *there she goes again.* It took some time and trouble, but eventually I learned to stop talking, to be (impersonate, really) an observer. This impersonation led me to write an enormous amount in the margins of my notebooks— marginalia I would later mine to make poems.

Forcing myself to shut up, pouring language onto paper instead: this became a habit. But now I've returned to copious speaking as well, in the form of teaching.

Sometimes, when I'm teaching, when I interject a comment without anyone calling on me, without caring that I just spoke a moment before, or when I interrupt someone to redirect the conversation away from an eddy I personally find fruitless, I feel high on the knowledge that I can talk as much as I want to, as quickly as I want to, in any direction that I want to, without anyone overtly rolling her eyes at me or suggesting I go to speech therapy. I'm not saying this is good pedagogy. I am saying that its pleasures are deep.

It's like she's pulling Post-it notes out of her hair and lecturing from them, one of my peers once complained about the teaching style of my beloved teacher Mary Ann Caws. I had to agree, this was an apt description of Caws's style (and hair). But not only did I love this style, I also loved it that no one could tell Caws to teach otherwise. You could abide her or drop her class: the choice was yours. Ditto Eileen Myles, who tells a great story about a student at UC San Diego once complaining that her lecturing style was like "throwing a pizza at us." My feeling is, you should be so lucky to get a pizza in the face from Eileen Myles, or a Post-it note plucked from the nest of Mary Ann Caws's hair.

Cordelia could not heave her heart into her mouth. Who can? No matter: her refusal to try famously becomes her badge of honor. But her silence has never moved me, quite; instead it's always struck me as a bit paranoid, sanctimonious—stingy, even.

Anne Carson *What exactly is lost to us when words are wasted?* Can it be that words comprise one of the few economies left on earth in which plenitude—surfeit, even—comes at no cost?

Recently I received in the mail a literary magazine that featured an interview with Anne Carson in which she answers certain questions—the boring ones? the too personal ones?—with empty brackets [[ ]]. There is something to learn here; I probably would have written a dissertation on each query, prompting the reply I've heard countless times in my life: "Really, it's terrific—it's just the people upstairs who say we've got to trim it back a little." The sight of Carson's brackets made me feel instantly ashamed of my compulsion to put my cards more decidedly on the table. But the more I thought about the brackets, the more they bugged me. They seemed to make a fetish of the unsaid, rather than simply letting it be contained in the sayable.

Many years ago, Carson gave a lecture at Teachers & Writers in New York City, at which she introduced (to me) the concept of leaving a space empty so that God could rush in. I knew a bit about this concept from my boyfriend at the time, who was big into bonsai. In bonsai you often plant the tree off-center in the pot to make space for the divine. But that night Carson made the concept literary. (*Act so that there is no use in a center:* a piece of Steinian wisdom Carson says she tries to impart to her students.) I had never heard of Carson before that night, but the room was packed and everyone else there clearly had. She gave a real lecture, with a Xeroxed slide list of Edward Hopper paintings and everything. She made being a professorial writer seem like the coolest thing you could ever be. I went home fastened to the concept of leaving the center empty for God. It was like stumbling into a tarot reading or AA meeting and hearing the one thing that will keep you going, in heart or art, for years.

Sitting now at my desk in my windowless office, its back wall painted pale blue in commemoration of the sky, I stare at the brackets in the Carson interview and try to enjoy them as markers of that evening from so long ago. But some revelations do not stand.

A student came to my office the other day and showed me an op-ed piece his mother had published in the *LA Times,* in which she describes her turbulent feelings about his transgender identity. "I want to love the man my daughter has become," the mother announces at the outset, "but floundering in the torrent of her change and my resistance to it, I fear I'll never make it across my river of anger and sorrow."

I talked with the student politely, then came home and raged, reading parts of the mother's op-ed aloud. "A transgender child brings a parent face to face with death," the mother laments. "The daughter I had known and loved was gone; a stranger with facial hair and a deep voice had taken her place." I couldn't tell what made me more upset—the terms with which the woman was talking about her child, or the fact that she had chosen to publish them in a major newspaper. I told you I was sick of stories in the mainstream media told by comfortably cisgendered folks—presumably "us"—expressing grief over the transitions of others, presumably "them." ("Where does it fit into the taxonomy of life crises when one person's liberation is another's loss?" Molly Haskell asks in her anguished account of her brother's MTF transition. In case her question is not rhetorical, I'd suggest the following answer: pretty damn low.)

To my surprise, you did not share my outrage. Instead, you raised an eyebrow and reminded me that, just a few years ago, I had expressed related fears, albeit not articulated in exactly the same terms, about the unknown changes that might be wrought by hormones, by surgery.

We were standing in our kitchen when you said this, at the same countertop where I suddenly remembered scouring the teeny print of a Canadian testosterone information pamphlet (Canada is light-years ahead of the United States on this front).

I had indeed been trying to figure out, in a sort of teary panic, what about you might change on T, and what would not.

By the time I was scouring the pamphlet, we'd been trying to get pregnant, without success, for over a year. I stayed busy trying to puff up my uterine lining by downing gobs of foul-smelling beige capsules and slick brown pellets from an acupuncturist with "a heavy hand," that is, one who left my legs covered with bruises; you had begun to lay the groundwork to have top surgery and start injecting T, which causes the uterus to shrivel. The surgery didn't worry me as much as the T—there's a certain clarity to excision that hormonal reconfiguration lacks— but part of me still wanted you to keep your chest the way it was. I wanted this for my sake, not yours (which meant it was a desire I would need to dispose of quickly). I also discovered that I harbored some unexamined butch bravado on your behalf, like—*You've had a beard for years and already pass 90 percent of the time without T, which is more than many folks who want such things can say; isn't that enough?*

Unable to say such things, I focused on the risks of elevated cholesterol and threats to your cardiovascular system that T might cause. My father died of a heart attack at age forty, for no sensible reason *("his heart exploded");* what if I lost you the same way? You were both Geminis. I read the risks aloud ominously, as if, once revealed, they might scare you off T for good. Instead you shrugged, reminded me that T would not put you in a higher risk category than that of bio males not on T. I sputtered a few half-baked Buddhist precepts about the potential unwisdom of making external changes rather than focusing on internal transformation. What if, once you made these big external changes, you still felt just as ill at ease in your body, in the world? *As if I did not know that, in the field of gender, there is no charting where the external and the internal begin and end—*

Exasperated, you finally said, *You think I'm not worried too? Of course I'm worried. What I don't need is your worry on top of mine. I need your support.* I get it, give it.

As it turned out, my fears were unwarranted. Which isn't to say you haven't changed. But the biggest change of all has been a measure of peace. The peace is not total, but in the face of a suffocating anxiety, a measure of peace is no small thing. You do feel grief-stricken now, but only that you waited so long, that you had to suffer so acutely for three decades before finally finding some relief. Which is why each time I count the four rungs down on the blue ladder tattooed on your lower back, spread out the skin, push in the nearly-two-inch-long needle, and plunge the golden, oily T into deep muscle mass, I feel certain I am delivering a gift.

And now, after living beside you all these years, and watching your wheel of a mind bring forth an art of pure wildness—as I labor grimly on these sentences, wondering all the while if prose is but the gravestone marking the forsaking of wildness (fidelity to sense-making, to assertion, to *argument,* however loose)—I'm no longer sure which of us is more at home in the world, which of us more free.

How to explain—"trans" may work well enough as shorthand, but the quickly developing mainstream narrative it evokes ("born in the wrong body," necessitating an orthopedic pilgrimage between two fixed destinations) is useless for some—but partially, or even profoundly, useful for others? That for some, "transitioning" may mean leaving one gender entirely behind, while for others—like Harry, who is happy to identify as a butch on T—it doesn't? *I'm not on my way anywhere,* Harry sometimes tells inquirers. How to explain, in a culture frantic for resolution, that sometimes the shit stays messy? *I do not want the female gender that has been assigned to me at birth. Neither do I want the male gender that transsexual medicine can furnish and that the state will award me if I behave in the right way. I don't want any of it.* How to explain that for some, or for some at some times, this irresolution is OK—desirable, even (e.g., "gender hackers")—whereas for others, or for others at some times, it stays a source of conflict or grief? How does one get across the fact that the best way to find out how people feel about their gender or their sexuality—or anything else, really—is to listen to what they tell you, and to try to treat them accordingly, without shellacking over their version of reality with yours?

Beatriz
Preciado

The *presumptuousness* of it all. On the one hand, the Aristotelian, perhaps evolutionary need to put everything into categories— *predator, twilight, edible*—on the other, the need to pay homage to the transitive, the flight, the great soup of being in which we actually live. *Becoming,* Deleuze and Guattari called this flight: becoming-animal, becoming-woman, becoming-molecular. A becoming in which one never becomes, a becoming whose rule is neither evolution nor asymptote but a certain turning, a certain turning inward, *turning into my own / turning on in / to my own self / at last / turning out of the / white cage, turning out of the / lady cage / turning at last.*

Lucille Clifton

It's painful for me that I wrote a whole book calling into question identity politics, only then to be constituted as a token of lesbian identity. Either people didn't really read the book, or the commodification

Butler

53

of identity politics is so strong that whatever you write, even when it's explicitly opposed to that politics, gets taken up by that machinery.

I think Butler is generous to name the diffuse "commodification of identity" as the problem. Less generously, I'd say that the simple fact that she's a lesbian is so blinding for some, that whatever words come out of her mouth—whatever words come out of *the lesbian's* mouth, whatever ideas spout from her head—certain listeners hear only one thing: *lesbian, lesbian, lesbian.* It's a quick step from there to discounting the lesbian—or, for that matter, anyone who refuses to slip quietly into a "postracial" future that resembles all too closely the racist past and present—as *identitarian,* when it's actually the listener who cannot get beyond the identity that he has imputed to the speaker. Calling the speaker *identitarian* then serves as an efficient excuse not to listen to her, in which case the listener can resume his role as speaker. And then we can scamper off to yet another conference with a keynote by Jacques Rancière, Alain Badiou, Slavoj Žižek, at which we can meditate on Self and Other, grapple with radical difference, exalt the decisiveness of the Two, and shame the unsophisticated identitarians, all at the feet of yet another great white man pontificating from the podium, just as we've done for centuries.

In response to a journalist who asked him to "summarize himself in a nutshell," John Cage once said, "Get yourself out of whatever cage you find yourself in." He knew his name was stuck to him, or he was stuck to it. Still, he urges out of it. The *Argo*'s parts may get replaced, but it's still called the *Argo*. We may become more used to jumping into flight, but that doesn't mean we have done with all perches. *We ought to say a feeling of and, a feeling of if, a feeling of but, and a feeling of by, quite as readily as we say a feeling of blue or a feeling of cold.* We ought

William James

to, but we don't—or at least, we don't quite as readily. But the more you do, the more quickly you can recognize the feeling when it comes around again, and hopefully you won't need to stare as long.

Throughout my twenties, I meditated weekly at the Russian & Turkish Baths on East Tenth Street on the impossibly ancient body of the woman whom I thought of as the ghost of the baths. (If you went to these baths on women-only days in the '90s, you will know who I mean.) I meditated on her labia, which drooped far below her pale pubic hair, her butt cheeks dangling off the bone like two deflated balloons. *And I said, do labia really start to hang? She said, yes, just like men's balls, gravity makes the labia hang. I told her I never noticed that, I'd have to take a look.* I tried to learn everything there was to know about the aging female body by staring at hers. (Now I realize I should say "the elderly female body," but in my youth, as in the culture at large, the space between "aging" and "elderly" women is often collapsed, treated as illegible or irrelevant.)

Dodie Bellamy

In my day job as a graduate student, however, I expressed only offense at Allen Ginsberg's descriptions of female genitalia in his poems, as in "the hang of pearplum / fat tissue / I had abhorred" and "the one hole that repelled me 1937 on." I still don't see the need to broadcast misogynistic repulsion, even in service of fagdom, but I do understand being repelled. Genitalia of all stripes are often slimy and pendulous and repulsive. That's part of their charm.

I realize now that such moments in Ginsberg have a different shine when held in the bowl alongside his go-for-broke encounter with the naked body of his mother, the mad Naomi, in his great "Kaddish":

One time I thought she was trying to make me come lay her—flirting to herself at sink—lay back on huge bed that filled most of the room, dress up round her hips, big slash of hair, scars of operations, pancreas, belly wounds, abortions, appendix, stitching of incisions pulling down in the fat like hideous thick zippers—ragged long lips between her legs—What, even, smell of asshole? I was cold—later revolted a little, not much—seemed perhaps a good idea to try—know the Monster of the Beginning Womb— Perhaps—that way. Would she care? She needs a lover.

Yisborach, v'yistabach, v'yispoar, v'yisroman, v'yisnaseh, v'yishador, v'yishalleh, v'yishallol, sh'meh d'kudsho, b'rich hu.

When I read this passage now, I feel only moved and inspired. "What, even, smell of asshole?"—this is the sound of Ginsberg cajoling himself as far out onto the ledge as he can go, even if it means pressing into the speculative, the fictive. Beyond the "Monster of the Beginning Womb" to the mother's anus, which he leans into and sniffs. Not in service of abjection, but in pursuit of the limits of generosity. *She needs a lover—am I that name?*

The result of all this pushing? "Later revolted a little, not much." O glorious deflation without dismissal!

I remember, around age ten, beholding the scene in *The Shining* in which the hot young woman whom Jack Nicholson is lewdly embracing in the haunted hotel bathroom ages rapidly in his arms, screeching from nubile chick to putrefying corpse within seconds. I understood that the scene was supposed to represent some kind of primal horror. This was *The Shining*, after all. But the image of that decaying, cackling crone, her arms outstretched in desire toward the man who is backing away, has stayed with me for three decades, as a type of friend. She's part baths-ghost, part mad-Naomi. She didn't get the memo about being beyond wanting or being wanted. Or perhaps she just means to scare the shit out of him, which she does.

At one point in her book *The Buddhist,* Dodie Bellamy takes Jonathan Franzen to task for the following description of a middle-aged woman found in his novel *Freedom:* "Then she waited, with parted lips and a saucy challenge in her eyes, to see how her presence—the drama of being her—was registering. In the way of such chicks, she seemed convinced of the originality of her provocation. Katz had encountered, practically verbatim, the same provocation a hundred times before, which put him in the ridiculous position now of feeling bad for being unable to pretend to be provoked: of pitying Lucy's doughty little ego, its flotation on a sea of aging-female insecurity." Bellamy responds: "Due to all the stagy point of view switches the novel apparently employs, I'd thought of assigning it to students, but after reading the above passage I was like, not in 100 fucking years. . . . Middle aged women are such easy prey, like they're supposed to walk around with eyes averted, hanging their heads in shame at their wreckage." She then offers "a sappy image of a crone to wipe out the evil Franzen-view."

I won't reproduce the image here, but I encourage you to find *The Buddhist* and consult it. What I will do is tell you about the stable of people I have come to think of as my sappy crones (except that they aren't really sappy, and they're not really crones). You've already met some of them. For a while I was calling them my good witches, but that wasn't quite right. If it weren't such a lengthy moniker I might call them "the many gendered-mothers of my heart," which is what poet Dana Ward calls everyone from Allen Ginsberg to Barry Manilow to his father to his grandmother to his childhood neighbor to Winona Ryder's character in *Heathers* to Ella Fitzgerald to Jacob von Gunten to his bio mom in his amazing long poem "A Kentucky of Mothers," which accomplishes the nearly impossible feat of constructing an ecstatic matriarchal cosmology while also defetishizing the maternal, even emptying the category out, eventually wondering: "But is 'mother of' precise? / Should I say 'singers of' instead? . . . Is it good to call these others as my moms the way I have? Is it care, & if it is have I gave honor in my song?"

My college professor of feminist theory was named Christina Crosby. I tried my very hardest in her class and she gave me an A-. I didn't get it then but now I do. I was cruising for intellectual mothers, unconsciously gravitating toward the stern and nonmaternal type. Christina would show up for class on her motorcycle or sleek road bike, blow into the room with her helmet under her arm, the whip of autumnal New England in her hair and cheeks, and everyone would quake with intimidation and desire. I always think of her entrances when I start a class now, as she always showed up just a smidgen late—never *actually* late, but never the first one to the party. She was radiant and elegant and butch, not stone and not soft, just her own blond, professorial, athletic, windswept kind of butch.

Christina, too, had a habit of blushing deep red while she spoke for the first few minutes of class. It didn't make her any less cool. In fact it made us think she ran hot on the inside, that something about her passion for Gayatri Spivak or the Combahee River Collective was uncontainable. And it was. Because of her blushing, I don't feel any substantive shame when this happens to me now, in the classroom. (It happens to me all the time.)

Eventually Christina and I became friends. A few years ago, she told me the story of a subsequent feminist theory class that threw a kind of coup. They wanted—in keeping with a long feminist tradition—a different kind of pedagogy than that of sitting around a table with an instructor. They were frustrated by the poststructuralist ethos of her teaching, they were tired of dismantling identities, tired of hearing that the most resistance one could muster in a Foucauldian universe was to work the trap one is inevitably in. So they staged a walkout and held class in a private setting, to which they invited Christina as a guest. When people arrived, Christina told me, a student handed everyone an index card and asked them to write "how they identified" on it, then pin it to their lapel.

Christina was mortified. Like Butler, she'd spent a lifetime complicating and deconstructing identity and teaching others to do the same, and now, as if in a tier of hell, she was being handed an index card and a Sharpie and being told to squeeze a Homeric epithet onto it. Defeated, she wrote "Lover of Babe." (Babe was her dog, a mischievous white lab.)

As she told me this story, I cringed all over—for the students, mostly, but also because I was remembering how, when I was Christina's student, we had all wanted her to come out in a more public and coherent fashion, and how frustrated we were that she wouldn't. (Actually, I wasn't all that frustrated; I've always sympathized with those who refuse to engage with terms or forums that feel like more of a compromise or distortion than an unbidden expression. But I understood why others were frustrated, and I sympathized with them, too.) Her students' frustration with her reticence about her personal life did not diminish their desire for her, however—sentiments such as "Christina Crosby's leather pants make me wet" appeared regularly on the cement paths all over campus. Likely her reticence but fed the fire. (Christina admitted to me later that she knew about the chalkings, and that they had pleased her very much.)

But as the times changed, Christina changed. She got together with a younger, more activist scholar who is more vocal about queer issues, about *being* queer. Like most academic feminists, Christina now teaches "gender and sexuality studies" rather than women's studies. Perhaps most moving to me, she is now writing autobiography—something she never would have dreamed of doing back when she was my mentor.

Back then, she said she was willing to be my thesis adviser because I struck her as serious, but she made it very clear that she felt no kinship—indeed, she felt a measure of repulsion—at my interest in the personal made public. I was ashamed, but undaunted (my epithet?). The thesis I produced under her tutelage was titled *The Performance of Intimacy.* I didn't mean the word *performance* in opposition to "the real"; I've never been interested in any sort of con. Of course there exist people who perform intimacy in ways that are fraudulent or narcissistic or dangerous or steamrolling or creepy, but that's not the kind of performance that I meant, or the kind I mean. I mean writing that dramatizes the ways in which we are _for another or by virtue of another,_ not in a single instance, but from the start and always.

Butler

When it comes to my own writing, if I insist that there is a persona or a performativity at work, I don't mean to say that I'm not myself in my writing, or that my writing somehow isn't me. I'm with Eileen Myles—"My dirty secret has always been that it's of course about me." Lately, however, I have felt myself awash in a fresh irony. After a lifetime of experimenting with the personal made public, each day that passes I watch myself grow more alienated from social media, the most rampant arena for such activity. Instantaneous, noncalibrated, digital self-revelation is one of my greatest nightmares. I feel quite certain that my character is too weak to withstand the temptations and pressures that would come with hoisting it onto the stage of Facebook, and truly amazed by the fact that so many others—or all others, so it sometimes seems—bear it so easily.

More than bear it—celebrate it, intrepidly push at its limits, just as they should. In *The Buddhist*—which was created from blog posts—Dodie Bellamy hails the blog of poet Jackie Wang, who once posted her thoughts as they decomposed under the influence of Ambien: "6am. hello. fading fast because i took an ambien and am becoming incoherent. but the nice thing about ambien is that you can write and write and write because you don't give a fuck, it;s good for the loosening that needs to happen in order to speak. . . . i was going to wrier sometrgiubf important but i snasccan6y cant read nmyg own handwriting and i hallucinate when i look at things." Intellectually, I'm right there with Dodie, cheering Jackie on. But in my heart I'm saying a prayer of gratitude: it was an act of grace that I got sober before I got wireless.

I haven't really thought this through (in homage to Wang?), but when I think about my more "personal" writing, I keep seeing that old Atari game, Breakout. I see the game's plain, flat cursor sliding around on the bottom of the screen, popping the little black dot back onto the thick bank of rainbow above. Each time the dot hits the bank, it eats away a chunk of color, until eventually it has eaten away enough of the bank to "break out." The breakout is a thrill because of all the triangulation, all the monotony, all the effort, all the obstruction, all the shapes and sounds that were its predecessor. I need those colored bricks to chip away at, because the eating into them makes form. And then I need the occasional jailbreak, my hypomanic dot riding the sky.

In Christina's feminist theory class we also read Irigaray's famous essay "When Our Lips Speak Together," in which Irigaray critiques both unitary and binary ways of thinking by focusing on the morphology of the labial lips. They are the "sex which is not one." They are not one, but also not two. They make a circle that is always self-touching, an autoerotic mandorla.

This image immediately struck me as weird but exciting. And a little embarrassing. It reminded me of the fact that a lot of women can jerk off just by pressing their legs together on a bus or in a chair or whatever (I came this way once while waiting in line to see *The Bitter Tears of Petra von Kant* at Film Forum on Houston). While we were discussing Irigaray in class, I tried to feel the circle of my labial lips. I imagined every woman in the class trying to feel it too. But the thing is, you can't really feel your labial lips.

It's easy to get juiced up about a concept like plurality or multiplicity and start complimenting everything as such. Sedgwick was impatient with that kind of sloppy praise. Instead, she spent a lot of time talking and writing about that which is more than one, and more than two, but less than infinity.

This finitude is important. It makes possible the great mantra, the great invitation, of Sedgwick's work, which is to "pluralize and specify." (Barthes: "one must pluralize, refine, continuously.") This is an activity that demands an attentiveness—a relentlessness, even—whose very rigor tips it into ardor.

A few months before Iggy was conceived, we went to see an art porn movie made by some friends, A. K. Burns and A. L.

Steiner. You were feeling lonely, longing for a sense of community, identification. Unlike the close-knit, DIY queer scene you were once at the center of in San Francisco, the queer scene in LA can feel like everything else in LA: partitioned by traffic and freeways, oppressively cliquish and bewilderingly diffuse at the same time, hard to fathom, to *see*.

The movie, *Community Action Center,* is pretty great. You liked its frenzied variety and absurdity, though you felt perplexed by its banishment of cock, as you think the category of women should be capacious enough to include it—"like the blob that ate Detroit," you say. I agreed, but wondered how to make space for the nonphallic if the phallic is always pushing its way back into the room. *In whose world are these terms mutually exclusive?* you said, justly agitated. *In whose world is the morphological imaginary defined as that which is not real?*

In one of my favorites of your drawings, two Popsicles are talking to each other. One accuses, "You're more interested in fantasy than reality." The other responds, "I'm interested in the reality of my fantasy." Both of the Popsicles are melting off their sticks.

After the movie had finished, the screen flashed a parting dedication: "to the queerest of the queer." The audience applauded, and I applauded too. But inside the dedication felt like a needle zigzagging off the record after a great song. Whatever happened to horizontality? Whatever happened to *the difference is spreading?* I tried to hold on to what I liked most about the movie, which was watching people hit each other during sex without it seeming violent, the scene of someone jerking off with a chunk of purple quartz down by the water, and the slow sewing of feathers onto a girl's butt. Really that's all I remember now. And that the girl having the feathers sewn onto her butt was pretty in an unusual way, and that her sexuality reminded me of mine in ways I couldn't name but that moved me. Those parts made that little portal swing open for me: *I think we have—and can have—a right to be free.*

Michel Foucault

I collect these moments. I know they hold a key. It doesn't matter to me if the key must remain perched in a lock, incipient. *The key is in the window, the key is in the sunlight at the window . . . the key is in the bars, in the sunlight in the window.*

Naomi Ginsberg, to Allen

Out in the lobby, a friend complains that the subtitle of the movie should have been "flip the butch" (presumably an insult), and is seriously grossed out by the sex. *Ugh, why did we have to stare at so many hairy pussies?* I drift off to the water fountain.

Like much of Catherine Opie's work, *Self-Portrait/Cutting* (1993), which features the bloody stick figures cut into her back, gains meaning in series, in context. Its crude drawing is in conversation with the ornate script of the word *Pervert,* which Opie had carved into the front of her chest and photographed a year later. And both are in conversation with the heterogeneous lesbian households of Opie's *Domestic* series (1995–98)—in which Harry appears, baby-faced—as well as with Opie's *Self-Portrait/ Nursing* (2004), taken a decade after *Self-Portrait/Pervert.* In Opie's nursing self-portrait, she holds and beholds her son Oliver while he nurses, her *Pervert* scar still visible, albeit ghosted, across her chest. The ghosted scar offers a rebus of sodomitical maternity: the pervert need not die or even go into hiding per se, but nor is adult sexuality foisted upon the child, made its burden.

This balance is admirable. It is also not always easy to maintain. In a recent interview, Opie says: "Between being a full-time professor and an artist and a mom and a partner, it's not like I get to have that much time to go and explore and play [SM style]. . . . Also, all of a sudden when you're taking care of a child, your brain doesn't easily switch to 'Oh, now I'm going to hurt somebody.'"

There is something profound here, which I will but draw a circle around for you to ponder. As you ponder, however, note that a difficulty in shifting gears, or a struggle to find the time, is not the same thing as an ontological either/or.

Of course, there are a multitude of good reasons for adults to keep their bodies to themselves, one of which is the simple aesthetic fact that adult bodies can be hideous to children. Listen, for example, to Hervé Guibert's description of his father's penis:

> I'm staring at his trousers as he opens his flies and that's when I see something I've never seen again in all my life: a kind of threshing ringed beast, cork-screwed and blood-filled and raw, a pink sausage ending in a cone-shaped knob. At this moment I see my father's prick as if it were skinless, as if my eyes had the power to see right through the flesh. I see something anatomically separate. It's as if I see a superimposed and scaled-down version of the shiny cosh that he brought back from the slaughterhouse and puzzlingly places on his bedside table.

This scene doesn't forecast damage or violation per se, but most such literary scenes (the non-French ones?) do. Think of *I Know Why the Caged Bird Sings,* by Maya Angelou, whose primal scene of violation I must have read a hundred times over as a young girl. Here is eight-year-old Maya, our narrator, reporting on the actions of her uncle: "Mr. Freeman pulled me to him, and put his hand between my legs. . . . He threw back the blankets and his 'thing' stood up like a brown ear of corn. He took my hand and said, 'Feel it.' It was mushy and squirmy like the inside of a freshly killed chicken. Then he dragged me on top of his chest." This is but the opening salvo of the recurring sexual abuse of Maya at the hands of Mr. Freeman.

To be honest, however, I didn't remember that the abuse continued until I researched it just now. As a child I stuttered out on just this one scene, so startled was I by the penis-corn.

If you're looking for sexual tidbits as a female child, and the only ones that present themselves depict child rape or other violations (all my favorite books in my preteen years: *I Know Why the Caged Bird Sings, Clan of the Cave Bear, The World According to Garp,* as well as the few R-rated movies I was allowed to see—*Fame,* most notably, with its indelible scene of Irene Cara being asked to take her shirt off and suck her thumb by a skeezy photographer who promises to make her a star), then your sexuality will form around that fact. There is no control group. I don't even want to talk about "female sexuality" until there is a control group. And there never will be.

In high school, a wise teacher assigned the short story "Wild Swans" by Alice Munro. The story blew through my penis-corn-addled mind and swept it clean. In just a few short pages, Munro lays it all out: how the force of one's adolescent curiosity and incipient lust often must war with the need to protect oneself from disgusting and wicked violators, how pleasure can coexist with awful degradation without meaning the degradation was justified or a species of wish fulfillment; how it feels to be both accomplice and victim; and how such ambivalences can live on in an adult sexual life. Munro makes "Wild Swans" more tolerable and interesting by having its protagonist get jerked off by a male stranger on a train (a traveling priest, of course) without her consent or protest, but also without her being forced to do anything to his body. In lieu of genital description, Munro gives us landscape: the view outside as the train hurtles forth, which the girl beholds as she comes.

When Iggy was five months old, we took him with us to one of my best friends' trapeze-burlesque shows, but were turned away at the door by a jovial Australian bouncer who told us that the show was 18+. I told him I wasn't worried about exposing the five-month-old strapped to my chest, asleep, to my best friend's foul mouth and naked body. He said the problem wasn't *my* baby per se—it was that other people would see the baby, and thereby be reminded of the babies they might have left at home, and it wouldn't feel to them like an adult night out. It would disrupt the cabaret atmosphere.

I'm all for adult nights out, and for cabaret atmospheres. This isn't a tract arguing for the right to carry a baby everywhere. I guess what annoyed me is that I wanted my friend to make the call, as she had invited us. Coming from the bouncer, I felt (paranoically? he was just doing his job) the specter of what Susan Fraiman has described as "a heroic gay male sexuality as a stand-in for queerness which remains 'unpolluted by procreative femininity.'"

To counter this stand-in, Fraiman expounds on the concept of sodomitical maternity, described at length in a chapter titled "In Search of the Mother's Anus," which wends through Freud's notorious Wolf Man case. A grown man in analysis (known to posterity as the Wolf Man) tells Freud about being a little boy—perhaps even a baby—and seeing his parents doing it "a tergo," or doggy-style, on multiple occasions. "The man upright, and the woman bent down like an animal." (It might be worth noting that this memory is pried out of the Wolf Man—it's not his calling card of complaint.) Freud says that the Wolf Man was "able to see his mother's genitals as well as his father's organ; and he understood the process as well as its significance." He also reports that the Wolf Man "assumed to begin with . . . that the event of which he was a witness was an act of violence, but the expression of enjoyment which he saw on his mother's face did not fit in with this; he was obliged to recognize that the experience was one of gratification."

When Freud goes to interpret the scene, however, the mother's genitals disappear. The mother becomes the "castrated wolf, which let the others climb upon it," and the father, the "wolf that climbed." This is no real surprise—as Winnicott has noted (along with Deleuze and others), Freud's career can sometimes seem a series of intoxications with theoretical concepts that willfully annihilate nuance. (Or reality: Freud later suggests that the boy may have seen sheepdogs copulating and hoisted the image onto his parents, and thus asks the reader "to join me in adopting a *provisional* belief in the reality of the scene." Such freely confessed swerves into the provisional are the pleasure of reading Freud; the problems come when he succumbs—or we succumb—to the temptation to mastery rather than reminding ourselves that we are at deep play in the makeshift.) In any event, at the time of his writing of Wolf Man, Freud's *plat du jour* was the castration complex. And this complex demands that the woman have "nothing," even in the face of testimony to the contrary.

Freud doesn't disappear the pleasure the Wolf Man notes on his mother's face, but he does twist it beyond recognition. He proposes that seeing the castrated mother get fucked in this way, and seeing her enjoy it, produces a primal, destabilizing fear in the Wolf Man, "which, in the form of concern for his male organ, was fighting against a satisfaction whose attainment seemed to involve the renunciation of that organ." Freud summarizes the psychic knot as follows: "'If you want to be sexually satisfied by Father,' we may perhaps represent [the Wolf Man] as saying to himself, 'you must allow yourself to be castrated like Mother; but I won't have that.'"

I won't have that: for Freud, the "that" is castration—clearly too large a price to pay for whatever pleasure may be at hand. For some queer theorists writing in Freud's wake, however, the "that" is something else entirely: the desire to be sexually satisfied by the father, in which case the penis is not renounced, but multiplied. This reading treats Wolf Man's memory of his parents' encounter "a tergo" as a primal, coded fantasy of gay male sex, a scene of proto-homosexuality. In which case, the Wolf Man's subsequent fear of his father is a fear not of castration, but of his own homosexual desire in a world that "won't have it."

Lee Edelman

This interpretation has appeal and value. But if the woman's genitals have to be willfully erased in order to get there, and her pleasure distorted into a cautionary tale re: the perils of castration, we have a problem. (Rule of thumb: when something needs to be willfully erased in order to get somewhere, there is usually a problem.) Thus, Fraiman aims to return the mother's pleasure to the scene, and to foreground her access—*"even as a mother"*—to "non-normative, nonprocreative sexuality, to sexuality in excess of the dutifully instrumental." The woman with such access and excess is the sodomitical mother.

Why did it take me so long to find someone with whom my perversities were not only compatible, but perfectly matched? Then as now, you spread my legs with your legs and push your cock into me, fill my mouth with your fingers. You pretend to use me, make a theater of heeding only your pleasure while making sure I find mine. Really, though, it's more than a perfect match, as that implies a kind of stasis. Whereas we're always moving, shape-shifting. No matter what we do, it always feels dirty without feeling lousy. Sometimes words are a part of it. I can remember, early on, standing beside you in a friend's cavernous fourth-floor painting studio in Williamsburg at night (she was out of town), completely naked, more construction workers outside, this time building some kind of luxury highrise across the street, their light towers flooding the studio with orange shaft and shadow, as you asked me to say aloud what I wanted you to do to me. My whole body struggled to summon any utterable phrase. I knew you were a good animal, but felt myself to be standing before an enormous mountain, a lifetime of unwillingness to claim what I wanted, to ask for it. Now here you were, your face close to mine, waiting. The words I eventually found may have been *Argo,* but now I know: there's no substitute for saying them with one's own mouth.

Sodomitical maternity was on full display in A. L. Steiner's 2012 installation *Puppies and Babies*—an anarchic, colorful, blissed-out collection of snapshots, culled from Steiner's personal archive, of friends in various states of public and private intimacy with the titular creatures. Steiner says the installation started as a kind of joke, the joke coming from "the fact that sometimes I'd find myself shooting puppies/dogs and babies and what for? Were they part of my 'work'? How did/ could they fit in to the highbrow genre of labels often attached to my work—installation-based, for mature audiences, political, etc?"

These are interesting questions. They did not occur to me, however, while beholding *Puppies and Babies*. I'd like to think this is because the dreary binary that would pit casual snapshots of "adorable" puppies and babies and their myriad caretakers and companions against "highbrow" genres of art has come to strike me as a malodorous missive from the mainstream: at times unavoidable, but best left unsniffed. (See the 2012 Mother's Day cover article in the *New York Times Book Review*, which began: "No subject offers a greater opportunity for terrible writing than motherhood. . . . To be fair, writing well about children is tough. You know why? They're not that interesting. What is interesting is that despite the mind-numbing boredom that constitutes 95 percent of child rearing, we continue to have them." Given that nearly every society on earth peddles the notion of having children as the ticket—perhaps the only ticket—to a meaningful life (all others being but a consolation prize)—and given that most have also devised all kinds of subtle to appalling ways to punish women who choose *not* to procreate—how could this latter proposition truly fascinate?)

Puppies and Babies is a terrific antidote to such sneering, with its joy-swirl of sodomitical parenthood, caretaking of all kinds, and interspecies love. In one photo, a naked woman spoons two dogs at once. In another, artist Celeste Dupuy-Spencer squats with her dog at the edge of a lake, as if both are contemplating a long journey. Babies get born, cry, goof around, ride small tractors, pinch nipples, get held. Often, they nurse. One nurses—incredibly—while the nursing mother does a handstand. Another nurses at the beach. Alex Auder, pregnant and in leather dom gear, pretends to give birth to an inflatable turtle. A dog mounts a stuffed tiger. Another dog is festooned with orange flowers. Two pregnant women hold up their sundresses to rub their naked bellies together, a friendly frottage.

Baby-lovers may gravitate to the baby photos, dog-lovers to the dogs, but the roughly equal wall space given to each places interspecies love firmly on par with human-human love. (Some photos feature both puppies and babies, in which case there's no need to choose.) And while there are a lot of pregnant bodies here, this orgy of adoration is clearly open to anyone who wants to play. Indeed, one of the gifts of genderqueer family making—and animal loving—is the revelation of caretaking as detachable from—and attachable to—any gender, any sentient being.

Beholding this celebration, I wonder if Fraiman's sodomitical maternity needs revision. It has been politically important for feminists to underplay the erotics of childbearing in order to make space for erotics elsewhere (i.e., "I fuck to come, not to conceive"), but *Puppies and Babies* eschews such cleavage. Instead we get all the messy, raucous perversities to be found in both pregnant and nonpregnant bodies, in nursing, in skinny-dipping in a waterfall with one's dog, in cavorting in crumpled bedsheets, in the daily work of caretaking and witness—including the erotic witness of Steiner's camera. (If you share Koestenbaum's happily prurient sentiment, "If I attend a photo show that lacks nudes, I consider the visit a waste," then you've come to the right place.)

Some of the subjects of *Puppies and Babies* may not identify as queer, but it doesn't matter: the installation queers them. By which I mean to say that it partakes in a long history of queers constructing their own families—be they composed of peers or mentors or lovers or ex-lovers or children or non-human animals—and that it presents queer family making as an umbrella category under which baby making might be a subset, rather than the other way around. It reminds us that any bodily experience can be made new and strange, that nothing we do in this life need have a lid crammed on it, that no one set of practices or relations has the monopoly on the so-called radical, or the so-called normative.

Homonormativity seems to me a natural consequence of the decriminalization of homosexuality: once something is no longer illicit, punishable, pathologized, or used as a lawful basis for raw discrimination or acts of violence, that phenomenon will no longer be able to represent or deliver on subversion, the subcultural, the underground, the fringe, in the same way. That's why nihilist pervs like painter Francis Bacon have gone so far as to say that they wish that the death penalty was still the punishment for homosexuality, or why outlaw fetishists like Bruce Benderson seek homosexual adventures in countries such as Romania, where one can still be imprisoned for merely hitting on someone of the same sex. "I still see homosexuality as a narrative of urban adventure, a chance to cross not only sex barriers but class and age barriers, while breaking a few laws in the process—and all for the sake of pleasure. If not, I might as well be straight," Benderson says.

In the face of such a narrative, it's a comedown to wade through the planet-killing trash of a Pride parade, or to hear Chaz Bono cluck-clucking with David Letterman about how T has made him kind of an asshole to his girlfriend, who still annoyingly wants him to "process" for hours in that dreaded lesbian/womanly way. I respect Chaz for many things, not the least of which is his willingness to speak his truth to an audience ready to revile him. But his eager (if strategic) identification with some of the worst stereotypes of straight men and lesbians is disappointing. ("Mission accomplished," Letterman declared sardonically in response.)

People are different from each other. Unfortunately, the dynamic of becoming a spokesperson almost always threatens to bury this fact. You may keep saying that you only speak for yourself, but your very presence in the public sphere begins to congeal difference into a single figure, and pressure begins to bear down hard upon it. Think of how freaked some people got when activist/actress Cynthia Nixon described her experience of her sexu-

ality as "a choice." But while *I can't change, even if I tried,* may be a true and moving anthem for some, it's a piss-poor one for others. At a certain point, the tent may need to give way to field.

Here is Catherine Opie, talking to *Vice* magazine:

> Interviewer: Well, I think you going from the SM scene to being a mom, and all your new photos are these blissful domestic scenes—that's shocking in a way, because people want to keep those kind of separate.

> Opie: They do want to keep it separate. So basically, becoming homogenized and part of mainstream domesticity is transgressive for somebody like me. Ha. That's a very funny idea.

Funny to her, maybe, but to those who are freaked out about the rise of homonormativity and its threat to queerness, not so much. But as Opie here implies, it's the binary of normative/transgressive that's unsustainable, along with the demand that anyone live a life that's all one thing.

The other day I heard a guy on the radio talking about prehistoric homes, and the particular way humans make home as opposed to, say, birds. It isn't a penchant for decoration that differentiates us—birds really have a corner on that—it's the compartmentalization of space. The way we cook and shit and work in different areas. We've done this forever, apparently.

This simple fact, gleaned from a radio program, suddenly put me at home in my species.

I've heard that, back in the day, Rita Mae Brown once tried to convince fellow lesbians to abandon their children in order to join the movement. But generally speaking, even in the most radical feminist and/or lesbian separatist circles, there have always been children around (Cherríe Moraga, Audre Lorde, Adrienne Rich, Karen Finley, Pussy Riot . . . the list could go on and on). Yet rather than fade away with the rise of queer parenthood of all stripes, the tired binary that places *femininity, reproduction, and normativity on one side and masculinity, sexuality, and queer resistance on the other* has lately reached a kind of apotheosis, often posing as a last, desperate stand against homo- and heteronormativity, both. In his polemic *No Future*, Lee Edelman argues that *"queerness* names the side of those *not* 'fighting for the children,' the side outside the consensus by which all politics confirms the absolute value of reproductive futurism." *Fuck the social order and the Child in whose name we're collectively terrorized; fuck Annie; fuck the waif from Les Mis; fuck the poor, innocent kid on the Net; fuck Laws both with capital ls and with small; fuck the whole network of Symbolic relations and the future that serves as its prop.* Or, to use a queer artist friend's more succinct slogan, *Don't produce and don't reproduce.*

Fraiman

Edelman

I know that Edelman is talking about the Child, not children per se, and that my artist friend is likely more concerned with jamming the capitalist status quo than with prohibiting the act of childbirth. And I too feel like jamming a stick in someone's eye every time I hear "protecting the children" as a rationale for all kinds of nefarious agendas, from arming kindergarten teachers to dropping a nuclear bomb on Iran to gutting all social safety nets to extracting and burning through what's left of the world's fossil fuel supply. But why bother fucking this Child when we could be fucking the specific forces that mobilize and crouch behind its image? Reproductive futurism needs no more disciples. But basking in the punk allure of "no future" won't suffice, either, as if all that's left for us to do is sit back and watch while the gratuitously wealthy and greedy shred our economy and our climate and our planet, crowing all the while about how lucky the jealous roaches are to get the crumbs that fall from their banquet. Fuck *them,* I say.

Perhaps due to my own issues with reproductive futurism, I've always been a little spooked by texts addressed to or dedicated to babies, be they unborn or infant. Such gestures are undoubtedly born from love, I know. But the illiteracy of the addressee—not to mention the temporal gap between the moment of the address and that at which the child will have grown into enough of an adult to receive it (presuming one ever becomes an adult, in relation to one's parents)—underscores the discomfiting fact that relation can never be achieved in a simple fashion through writing, if it can be achieved at all. It frightens me to involve a tiny human being in this difficulty, this misfiring, from the start. And yet certain instances have undeniably moved me, such as André Breton's letter to his infant daughter in *Mad Love.* Breton's hetero romanticism is, as always, hard to take. But I like the sweet assurance he offers his daughter, that she was "thought of as possible, as certain, in the very moment when, in a love deeply sure of itself, a man and a woman wanted you to be."

Insemination after insemination, wanting our baby to be. Climbing up on the cold exam table, abiding the sting of the catheter threaded through the opal slit of my cervix, feeling the familiar cramp of rinsed, thawed seminal fluid pooling directly into my uterus. You holding my hand month after month, in devotion, in perseverance. *They're probably shooting egg whites,* I said, tears sprouting. *Shhh,* you whispered. *Shhh.*

The first few times we did the procedure, I brought a satchel of good luck charms. Sometimes, after the nurse dimmed the lights and left the room, you would hold me as I made myself come. The point wasn't romance as much as it was to suck the specimen upward (even though we knew it was already about as far up as it could go). As the months went by, however, I started leaving the charms at home. Eventually I felt lucky if I made it to the class I was teaching with the right book in my hand, so scrambled had I become by all the early-morning temperature taking, impossible-to-read ovulation predictor kits, the tortuous examination of every "spin-like" excretion that exited my body, the sharp despair wrought by the first smudge of menstrual blood.

Frustrated with our costly, ineffective approach, we off-roaded for a few months with a noble friend who generously agreed to be our donor, trading the cold metal table for the comfort of our bed, and pricey vials for our friend's free specimen, which he would leave in our bathroom in a squat glass jar that used to hold Paul Newman salsa.

One month our donor friend tells us that he has to go out of town for a college reunion. Not wanting to lose the month's egg, we trudge back to the bank. We track the egg's progress via ultrasound: it looks bulbous and beautiful and ready to burst out of its follicle in the late afternoon, but by the next morning there is no sign of it, not even a trace of fluid from its ruptured sac. I am beyond frustrated, beyond hope. But Harry—always the optimist!—insists it might not be too late. The nurse concurs. Knowing that I have a bad habit of deeming myself lost and getting off the freeway one exit before I would have found my way, I decide, once again, to join them.

Julia Kristeva *[Single or lesbian motherhood] can be seen as [one] of the most violent forms taken by the rejection of the symbolic . . . as well as one of the most fervent divinizations of maternal power—all of which cannot help but trouble an entire legal and moral order without, however, proposing an alternative to it.*

Given that one-third of American families are currently headed by single mothers (the census doesn't even ask about two mothers or any other forms of kinship—if there is anyone in the house called mother and no father, then your household counts as single mother), you'd think the symbolic order would be showing a few more dents by now. But Kristeva is not alone in her hyperbole. For a more disorienting take on the topic, I recommend Jean Baudrillard's "The Final Solution," in which Baudrillard argues that assisted forms of reproduction (donor insemination, surrogacy, IVF, etc.), along with the use of contraception, herald the suicide of our species, insofar as they detach reproduction from sex, thus turning us from "mortal, sexed beings" into clone-like messengers of an impossible immortality. So-called artificial insemination, Baudrillard argues, is linked with "the abolition of everything within us that is human, all too human: our desires, our deficiencies, our neuroses, our dreams, our disabilities, our viruses, our lunacies, our unconscious and even our sexuality—all the features which make us specific living beings."

Honestly I find it more embarrassing than enraging to read Baudrillard, Žižek, Badiou, and other revered philosophers of the day pontificating on how we might save ourselves from the humanity-annihilating threat of the turkey baster (which no one uses, by the way; the preferred tool is an oral syringe) in order to protect the fate of this endangered "sexed being." And by sexed, make no mistake: they mean one of two options. Here's Žižek, describing the type of sexuality that would fit an "evil" world: "In December 2006 the New York City authorities declared that the right to chose one's gender (and so, if necessary, to have the sex-change operation performed) is one of the inalienable human rights—the ultimate Difference, the 'transcendental' difference that grounds the very human identity, thus turns into something open to manipulation. . . . 'Masturbathon' is the ideal form of the sex activity of this trans-gendered subject."

Fatally estranged from the transcendental difference that grounds human identity, the transgendered subject is barely human, condemned forever to "idiotic masturbatory enjoyment" in lieu of the "true love" that renders us human. For, as Žižek holds—in homage to Badiou—"it is love, the encounter of the Two, which 'transubstantiates' the idiotic masturbatory enjoyment into an event proper."

These are the voices that pass for radicality in our times. Let us leave them to their love, their event proper.

2011, the summer of our changing bodies. Me, four months pregnant, you six months on T. We pitched out, in our inscrutable hormonal soup, for Fort Lauderdale, to stay for a week at the beachside Sheraton in monsoon season, so that you could have top surgery by a good surgeon and recover. Less than twenty-four hours after we arrived, they were snapping a sterile green hat on your head—a "party hat," the nice nurse said—and wheeling you away. While you were under the knife, I drank gritty hot chocolate in the waiting room and watched Diana Nyad try to swim from Florida to Cuba. She didn't make it that time, even in her shark cage. But you did. You emerged four hours later, hilariously zonked from the drugs, trying in vain to play the host while slipping in and out of consciousness, your whole torso more tightly bound than you've ever managed yourself, a drain hanging off each side, two pouches that filled up over and over again with blood stuff the color of cherry Kool-Aid.

To save money over the week, we cooked our food in the hotel bathroom on a hot plate. One day we drove to a Sport Chalet and bought a little tent to set up on the beach because the beachside cabanas cost too much money to rent. While you slept I ambled down to the beach and set up the tent, then tried to read Sedgwick's *A Dialogue on Love* inside. But it was like a nylon sweat lodge in there, and neither I nor the four-month-old fetus could tolerate it. I had started showing, which was delightful. Maybe there would be a baby. One night we splurged in our sober way and had eight-dollar virgin strawberry daiquiris at the infinity pool, which was stocked with Europeans on cheap vacation packages. The air was hot and lavender with a night storm coming in. There was always a storm coming in. Frat brothers and sorority sisters thronged every fried fish joint on the boardwalk. The crowds were loud and repulsive and a little scary but we were protected by our force field. On our third day, we drove to the second-largest mall in the world and walked for hours, even though I was dizzy and exhausted from early pregnancy and the suffocating heat and you were just barely over the lip of the Vicodin. At the mall I went into Motherhood Maternity and tried on clothes with one of those gelatin strap-on bellies they have so you can see what you'll look like as you grow big. Wearing the strap-on belly, I tried on a fuzzy white wool sweater with a bow at the sternum, the kind that makes your baby look like a present. I bought the sweater and ended up wearing it back at home all winter. You bought some loungy Adidas pants that look hot on you. Over and over again we emptied your drains into little Dixie cups and flushed the blood stuff down the hotel toilet. I've never loved you more than I did then, with your Kool-Aid drains, your bravery in going under the knife to live a better life, a life of wind on skin, your nodding off while propped up on a throne of hotel pillows, so as not to disturb your stitches. "The king's sleep," we called it, in homage to our first pay-per-view purchase of the week, *The King's Speech*.

Later, from our Sheraton Sweet Sleeper® Bed, we ordered *X-Men: First Class*. Afterward we debated: assimilation vs. revolution. I'm no cheerleader for assimilation per se, but in the movie the assimilationists were advocating nonviolence and identification with the Other in that bastardized Buddhist way that gets me every time. You expressed sympathy for the revolutionaries, who argued, *Stay freaky and blow 'em up before they come for you, because no matter what they say, the truth is they want you dead, and you're fooling yourself if you think otherwise.*

Professor: I can't stop thinking about the others out there, all those minds that I touched. I could feel them, their isolation, their hopes, their ambitions. I tell you we can start something incredible, Erik. We can help them.

Erik Lehnsherr: Can we? Identification, that's how it starts. And ends with being rounded up, experimented on and eliminated.

Professor: Listen to me very carefully, my friend: killing Shaw will not bring you peace.

Erik Lehnsherr: Peace was never an option.

We bantered good-naturedly, yet somehow allowed ourselves to get polarized into a needless binary. That's what we both hate about fiction, or at least crappy fiction—it purports to provide occasions for thinking through complex issues, but really it has predetermined the positions, stuffed a narrative full of false choices, and hooked you on them, rendering you less able to see out, to *get* out.

While we talked we said words like *nonviolence, assimilation, threats to survival, preserving the radical.* But when I think about it now I hear only the background buzz of our trying to explain something to each other, to ourselves, about our lived experiences thus far on this peeled, endangered planet. As is so often the case, the intensity of our need to be understood distorted our positions, backed us further into the cage.

Do you want to be right or do you want to connect? ask couples' therapists everywhere.

Deleuze/Parnet *The aim is not to answer questions, it's to get out, to get out of it.*

Flipping channels on a different day, we landed on a reality TV show featuring a breast cancer patient recovering from a double mastectomy. It was uncanny to watch her performing the same actions we were performing—emptying her drains, waiting patiently for her unbinding—but with opposite emotions. You felt unburdened, euphoric, reborn; the woman on TV feared, wept, and grieved.

Our last night at the Sheraton, we have dinner at the astoundingly overpriced "casual Mexican" restaurant on the premises, Dos Caminos. You pass as a guy; I, as pregnant. Our waiter cheerfully tells us about his family, expresses delight in ours. On the surface, it may have seemed as though your body was becoming more and more "male," mine, more and more "female." But that's not how it felt on the inside. On the inside, we were two human animals undergoing transformations beside each other, bearing each other loose witness. In other words, we were aging.

Many women describe the feeling of having a baby come out of their vagina as taking the biggest shit of their lives. This isn't really a metaphor. The anal cavity and vaginal canal lean on each other; they, too, are the sex which is not one. Constipation is one of pregnancy's principal features: the growing baby literally deforms and squeezes the lower intestines, changing the shape, flow, and plausibility of one's feces. In late pregnancy, I was amazed to find that my shit, when it would finally emerge, had been deformed into Christmas tree ornament–type balls. Then, all through my labor, I could not shit at all, as it was keenly clear to me that letting go of the shit would mean the total disintegration of my perineum, anus, and vagina, all at once. I also knew that if, or when, I could let go of the shit, the baby would probably come out. But to do so would mean *falling forever, going to pieces.*

In perusing the Q&A sections of pregnancy magazines at my ob/gyn's office before giving birth, I learned that a surprising number of women have a related but distinct concern about shit and labor (either that, or the magazine editors are making it up, as a kind of projective propaganda):

Q: If my husband watches me labor, how will he ever find me sexy again, now that he's seen me involuntarily defecate, and my vagina accommodate a baby's head?

This question confused me; its description of labor did not strike me as exceedingly distinct from what happens during sex, or at least some sex, or at least much of the sex I had heretofore taken to be good.

No one asked, *How does one submit to falling forever, to going to pieces.* A question from the inside.

In current "grrrl" culture, I've noted the ascendancy of the phrase "I need X like I need a dick in my ass." Meaning, of course, that X is precisely what you *don't* need (dick in my ass = hole in my head = fish with a bicycle, and so on). I'm all for girls feeling empowered to reject sexual practices that they don't enjoy, and God knows many straight boys are all too happy to stick it in any hole, even one that hurts. But I worry that such expressions only underscore the "ongoing absence of a discourse of female anal eroticism . . . the flat fact that, since classical times, *there has been no important and sustained Western discourse in which women's anal eroticism means.* Means anything."

Sedgwick

Sedgwick did an enormous amount to put women's anal eroticism on the map (even though she was mostly into spanking, which is not precisely an anal pursuit). But while Sedgwick (and Fraiman) want to make space for women's anal eroticism to *mean,* that is not the same as inquiring into how it *feels.* Even ex-ballerina Toni Bentley, who knocked herself out to become the culture's go-to girl for anal sex in her memoir *The Surrender,* can't seem to write a sentence about ass-fucking without obscuring it via metaphor, bad puns, or spiritual striving. And

Fraiman exalts the female anus mostly for what it is not: the vagina (presumably a lost cause, for the sodomite).

I am not interested in a hermeneutics, or an erotics, or a metaphorics, of my anus. I am interested in ass-fucking. I am interested in the fact that the clitoris, disguised as a discrete button, sweeps over the entire area like a manta ray, impossible to tell where its eight thousand nerves begin and end. I am interested in the fact that the human anus is one of the most innervated parts of the body, as Mary Roach explained to Terry Gross in a perplexing piece of radio that I listened to while driving Iggy home from his twelve-month vaccinations. I checked on Iggy periodically in the rearview mirror for signs of a vaccine-induced neuromuscular breakdown while Roach explained that the anus has "tons of nerves. And the reason is that it needs to be able to discriminate, by feel, between solid, liquid and gas and be able to selectively release one or maybe all of those. And thank heavens for the anus because, you know, really a lot of gratitude, ladies and gentlemen, to the human anus." To which Gross replied: "Let's take a short break here, then we'll talk some more. This is *Fresh Air.*"

A few months after Florida: you always wanting to fuck, raging with new hormones and new comfort in your skin; me vaulting fast into the unfuckable, not wanting to dislodge the hard-won baby seed, falling through the bed with dizziness whenever I turned my head—*falling forever*—all touch starting to sicken, as if the cells of my skin were individually nauseated.

That hormones can make the feel of wind, or the feel of fingers on one's skin, change from arousing to nauseating is a mystery deeper than I can track or fathom. The mysteries of psychology pale in comparison, just as evolution strikes me as infinitely more spiritually profound than Genesis.

Our bodies grew stranger, to ourselves, to each other. You sprouted coarse hair in new places; new muscles fanned out across your hip bones. My breasts were sore for over a year, and while they don't hurt anymore, they still feel like they belong to someone else (and in a sense, since I'm still nursing, they do). For years you were stone; now you strip your shirt off whenever you feel like it, emerge muscular, shirtless, into public spaces, go running—swimming, even.

Via T, you've experienced surges of heat, an adolescent budding, your sexuality coming down from the labyrinth of your mind and disseminating like a cottonwood tree in a warm wind. You like the changes, but also feel them as a sort of compromise, a wager for visibility, as in your drawing of a ghost who proclaims, *Without this sheet, I would be invisible.* (Visibility makes possible, but it also disciplines: disciplines gender, disciplines genre.) Via pregnancy, I have my first sustained encounter with the pendulous, the slow, the exhausted, the disabled. I had always presumed that giving birth would make me feel invincible and ample, like fisting. But even now—two years out—my insides feel more quivery than lush. I've begun to give myself over to the idea that the sensation might be forever changed, that this sensitivity is now mine, ours, to work with. Can fragility feel as hot as bravado? I think so, but sometimes struggle to find the way. Whenever I think I can't find it, Harry assures me that we can. And so we go on, our bodies finding each other again and again, even as they—we—have also been *right here,* all along.

For reasons almost incomprehensible to me now, I cried a little when our first ultrasound technician—the nice, seemingly gay Raoul, who sported a little silver sperm-squiggle pin on his white coat—told us at twenty weeks that our baby was a boy, without a shadow of a doubt. I guess I had to mourn something—the fantasy of a feminist daughter, the fantasy of a mini-me. Someone whose hair I could braid, someone who might serve as a femme ally to me in a house otherwise occupied by an adorable boy terrier, my beautiful, swaggery stepson, and a debonair butch on T.

But that was not my fate, nor was it the baby's. Within twenty-four hours of hearing the news, I was on board. Little Agnes would be little Iggy. And I would love him fiercely. Maybe I would even braid his hair! As you reminded me on the drive home from our appointment, *Hey, I was born female, and look how that turned out.*

Despite agreeing with Sedgwick's assertion that "women and men are more like each other than chalk is like cheese, than ratiocination is like raisins, than up is like down, or than 1 is like 0," it took me by surprise that my body could make a male body. Many women I know have reported something of the same, even though they know this is the most ordinary of miracles. As my body made the male body, I felt the difference between male and female body melt even further away. I was making a body with a difference, but a girl body would have been a different body too. The principal difference was that the body I made would eventually slide out of me and be its own body. Radical intimacy, radical difference. Both in the body, both in the bowl.

I kept thinking then about something poet Fanny Howe once said about bearing biracial children, something about how you become what grows inside you. But however "black" Howe might have felt herself becoming while gestating her children, she also remained keenly aware that the outside world was ready and waiting—and all too willing—to reinforce the color divide. She is of her children, and they are of her. But they know and she knows they do not share the same lot.

This divide provoked in Howe the sensation of being a double agent, especially in all-white settings. She recalls how, at gatherings in the late '60s, white liberals would openly converse "about their fear of blacks, and their judgments of blacks, and I had to announce to them that my husband and children were black, before hastily departing." This scene was not limited to the '60s. "This event has been repeated so many times, in multiple forms, that by now I make some kind of give-away statement after entering a white-only room, one way or the other, that will warn the people there 'which side I am on,'" Howe says. "On these occasions, more than any others, I feel that my skin is white but my soul is not, and that I am in camouflage."

Harry lets me in on a secret: guys are pretty nice to each other in public. Always greeting each other "hey boss" or nodding as they pass each other on the street.

Women aren't like that. I don't mean that women are all backstabbers or have it in for each other or whatnot. But in public, we don't nod nobly at each other. Nor do we really need to, as that nod also means *I mean you no violence.*

Over lunch with a fag friend of ours, Harry reports his findings about male behavior in public. Our friend laughs and says: *Maybe if I looked like Harry, I'd get a "hey boss" too!*

When a guy has cause to stare at Harry's driver's license or credit card, there comes an odd moment during which their camaraderie as two dudes screeches to a halt. The friendliness can't evaporate on a dime, however, especially if there has been a longish prior interaction, as one might have over the course of a meal, with a waiter.

Recently we were buying pumpkins for Halloween. We'd been given a little red wagon to put our pumpkins in as we traipsed around the field. We'd haggled over the price, we'd ooed and ahed at the life-sized mechanical zombie removing his head. We'd been given freebie minipumpkins for our cute baby. Then, the credit card. The guy paused for a long moment, then said, "This is her card, right?"—pointing at me. I almost felt sorry for him, he was so desperate to normalize the moment. I should have said yes, but I was worried I would open up a new avenue of trouble (*never the scofflaw*—yet I know I have what it takes to put my body on the line, if and when it comes down to it; this knowledge is a hot red shape inside me). We just froze in the way we freeze until Harry said, "It's my card." Long pause, sidelong stare. A shadow of violence usually drifts over the scene. "It's complicated," Harry finally said, puncturing the silence. Eventually, the man spoke. "No, actually, it's not," he said, handing back the card. "Not complicated at all."

Every other weekend of my pregnant fall—my so-called golden trimester—I traveled alone around the country on behalf of my book *The Art of Cruelty*. Quickly I realized that I would need to trade in my prideful self-sufficiency for a willingness to ask for help—in lifting my bags in and out of overhead compartments, up and down subway steps, and so on. I received this help, which I recognized as great kindness. On more than one occasion, a service member in the airport literally saluted me as I shuffled past. Their friendliness was nothing short of shocking. *You are holding the future; one must be kind to the future* (or at least a certain image of the future, which I apparently appeared able to deliver, and our military ready to defend). So this is the seduction of normalcy, I thought as I smiled back, compromised and radiant.

But the pregnant body in public is also obscene. It radiates a kind of smug autoeroticism: an intimate relation is going on—one that is visible to others, but that decisively excludes them. Service members may salute, strangers may offer their congratulations or their seats, but this privacy, this bond, can also irritate. It especially irritates the antiabortionists, who would prefer to pry apart the twofer earlier and earlier—twenty-four weeks, twenty weeks, twelve weeks, six weeks . . . The sooner you can pry the twofer apart, the sooner you can dispense with one constituent of the relationship: *the woman with rights.*

For all the years I didn't want to be pregnant—the years I spent harshly deriding "the breeders"—I secretly felt pregnant women were smug in their complaints. Here they were, sitting on top of the cake of the culture, getting all the kudos for doing exactly what women are supposed to do, yet still they felt unsupported and discriminated against. Give me a break! Then, when I wanted to be pregnant but wasn't, I felt that pregnant women had the cake I wanted, and were busy bitching about the flavor of the icing.

I was wrong on all counts—imprisoned, as I was and still am, by my own hopes and fears. I'm not trying to fix that wrongness here. I'm just trying to let it *hang out.*

Place me now, like a pregnant cutout doll, at a "prestigious New York university," giving a talk on my book on cruelty.

During the Q&A, a well-known playwright raises his hand and says: *I can't help but notice that you're <u>with child</u>, which leads me to the question—how did you handle working on all this dark material [sadism, masochism, cruelty, violence, and so on] in your <u>condition</u>?*

Ah yes, I think, digging a knee into the podium. Leave it to the old patrician white guy to call the lady speaker back to her body, so that no one misses the spectacle of that wild oxymoron, *the pregnant woman who thinks.* Which is really just a pumped-up version of that more general oxymoron, *a woman who thinks.*

As if anyone was missing the spectacle anyway. As if a similar scene didn't recur at nearly every location of my so-called book tour. As if when I myself see pregnant women in the public sphere, there isn't a kind of drumming in my mind that threatens to drown out all else: *pregnant, pregnant, pregnant,* perhaps because the soul (or souls) in utero is pumping out static, static that disrupts our usual perception of an other as a *single* other. The static of facing not one, but also not two.

During irritating Q&As, bumpy takeoffs and landings, and frightful faculty meetings, I placed my hands on my risen belly and attempted silent communion with the being spinning in the murk. Wherever I went, there the baby went, too. Hello New York! Hello bathtub! And yet babies have a will of their own, which becomes visible the first time mine sticks out a limb and makes a tent of my belly. During the night he gets into weird positions, forcing me to plead, *Move along, little baby! Get your foot off my lungs!* And if you are tracking a problem, as I was, you may have to watch the baby's body develop in ways that might harm him, with nothing you can do about it. Powerlessness, finitude, endurance. You are making the baby, but not *directly*. You are responsible for his welfare, but unable to control the core elements. You must allow him to unfurl, you must feed his unfurling, you must hold him. But he will unfurl as his cells are programmed to unfurl. You can't reverse an unfolding structural or chromosomal disturbance by ingesting the right organic tea.

Why do we have to measure his kidneys and freak out about their size every week if we've already decided we are not going to take him out early or do anything to treat him until after he's born? I asked the doctor rolling the sticky ultrasound shaft over my belly for seemingly the thousandth time. *Well, most mothers want to know as much as possible about the condition of their babies,* she said, avoiding my eyes.

Truth be told, when we first started trying to conceive, I had hoped to be done with my cruelty project and onto something "cheerier," so that the baby might have more upbeat accompaniment in utero. But I needn't have worried—not only did getting pregnant take much longer than I'd wanted it to, but pregnancy itself taught me how irrelevant such a hope was. Babies grow in a helix of hope and fear; gestating draws one but deeper into the spiral. It isn't cruel in there, but it's dark. I would have explained this to the playwright, but he had already left the room.

After the Q&A at this event, a woman came up to me and told me that she just got out of a relationship with a woman who had wanted her to hit her during sex. *She was so fucked up,* she said. *Came from a background of abuse. I had to tell her I couldn't do that to her, I could never be that person.* She seemed to be asking me for a species of advice, so I told her the only thing that occurred to me: I didn't know this other woman, so all that seemed clear to me was that their perversities were not compatible.

Even identical genital acts mean very different things to different people. This is a crucial point to remember, and also a difficult one. It reminds us that there is difference right where we may be looking for, and expecting, communion.

Sedgwick

At twenty-eight weeks, I was hospitalized for some bleeding. While discussing a possible placental issue, one doctor quipped, "We don't want that, because while that would likely be OK for the baby, it might not be OK for you." By pressing a bit, I figured out that she meant, in that particular scenario, the baby would likely live, but I might not.

Now, I loved my hard-won baby-to-be fiercely, but I was in no way ready to bow out of this vale of tears for his survival. Nor do I think those who love me would have looked too kindly on such a decision—a decision that doctors elsewhere on the globe are mandated to make, and that the die-hard antiabortionists are going for here.

Once I was riding in a cab to JFK, passing by that amazingly overpacked cemetery along the Brooklyn-Queens Expressway (Calvary?). My cabdriver gazed out wistfully at the headstones packed onto the hill and said, *Many of those graves are the graves of children. Likely so,* I returned with a measure of fatigued trepidation, the result of years of fielding unwanted monologues from cabdrivers about how women should live or behave. *It is a good thing when children die,* he said. *They go straight to Paradise, because they are the innocents.*

During my sleepless night under placental observation, this monologue came back to me. And I wondered if, instead of working to fulfill the dream of worldwide enforced childbearing, abortion foes could instead get excited about all the innocent, unborn souls going straight from the abortion table to Paradise, no detour necessary into this den of iniquity, which eventually makes whores of us all (not to mention Social Security recipients). Could that get them off our backs once and for all?

Never in my life have I felt more prochoice than when I was pregnant. And never in my life have I understood more thoroughly, and been more excited about, a life that began at conception. Feminists may never make a bumper sticker that says IT'S A CHOICE AND A CHILD, but of course that's what it is, and we know it. We don't need to wait for George Carlin to spill the beans. We're not idiots; we understand the stakes. Sometimes we choose death. Harry and I sometimes joke that women should get way beyond twenty weeks—maybe even up to two days after birth—to decide if they want to keep the baby. (Joke, OK?)

I have saved many mementos for Iggy, but I admit to tossing away an envelope with about twenty-five ultrasound photos of his in-utero penis and testicles, which a chirpy, blond ponytailed technician printed out for me every time I had an ultrasound. *Boy, he's sure proud of his stuff,* she would say, before jabbing Print. Or, *He really likes to show it off!*

Just let him wheel around in his sac for Christ's sake, I thought, grimly folding the genital triptychs into my wallet, week after week. Let him stay oblivious—for the first and last time, perhaps—to the task of performing a self for others, to the fact that we develop, even in utero, in response to a flow of projections and reflections ricocheting off us. Eventually, we call that snowball a self (*Argo*).

I guess the cheery way of looking at this snowball would be to say, subjectivity is keenly relational, and it is strange. *We are for another, or by virtue of another.* In my final weeks, I walked every day in the Arroyo Seco, listing aloud all the people who were waiting on earth to love Iggy, hoping that the promise of their love would eventually be enough to lure him out.

As my due date neared, I confided in Jessica, the woman who would be assisting our birth, that I was worried I wouldn't be able to make milk, as I had heard of women who couldn't. She smiled and said, *You've made it already.* Seeing me unconvinced, she said, *Want me to show you?* I nodded, shyly lifting a breast out of my bra. In one stunning gesture, she took my breast into her hand-beak and clamped down hard. A bloom of custard-colored drops rose in a ring, indifferent to my doubts.

According to Kaja Silverman, the turn to a paternal God comes on the heels of the child's recognition that the mother cannot protect against all harm, that her milk—be it literal or figurative—doesn't solve all problems. As the human mother proves herself a separate, finite entity, she disappoints, and gravely. In its rage at maternal finitude, the child turns to an all-powerful patriarch—God—who, by definition, cannot let anyone down. "The extraordinarily difficult task imposed upon the child's primary caretaker not only by the culture but also by Being itself is to induct it into relationality by saying over and over again, in a multitude of ways, what death will otherwise have to teach it: 'This is where you end and others begin.'

Unfortunately, this lesson seldom 'takes,' and the mother usually delivers it at enormous cost to herself. Most children respond to the partial satisfaction of their demands with extreme rage, rage that is predicated on the belief that the mother is withholding something that is within her power to provide."

I get that if the caretaker does not teach the lesson of the "me" and the "not-me" to the child, she may not make adequate space for herself. But why does the delivery of this lesson come at such an enormous cost? What is the cost? Withstanding a child's rage? Isn't a child's rage something we should be able to withstand?

Silverman also contends that a baby's demands on the mother can be "very flattering to the mother's narcissism, since it attributes to her the capacity to satisfy her infant's lack, and so— by extension—her own. Since most women in our culture are egoically wounded, the temptation to bathe in the sun of this idealization often proves irresistible." I have seen some mothers use their babies to fill a lack, or soothe an egoic wound, or bathe in the sun of idealization in ways that seemed pathological. But for the most part those people were pathological prior to having a baby. They would have had a pathological relation to carrot juice. Remnant Lacanian that she is, Silverman's aperture does not seem wide enough to include an enjoyment that doesn't derive from filling a void, or love that is not merely balm for a wound. So far as I can tell, most worthwhile pleasures on this earth slip between gratifying another and gratifying oneself. Some would call that an ethics.

Silverman does imagine, however, that this cycle could or should change: "Our culture should support [the mother] by providing enabling representations of maternal finitude, but instead it keeps alive in all of us the tacit belief that [the mother] *could* satisfy our desires if she really *wanted to.*" What would these "enabling representations" look like? Better parts for women in Hollywood movies? Books like this one? I don't want to represent anything.

At the same time, every word that I write could be read as some kind of defense, or assertion of value, of whatever it is that I am, whatever viewpoint it is that I ostensibly have to offer, whatever I've lived. *You know so much about people from* Eileen Myles *the second they open their mouths. Right away you might know that you might want to keep them out.* That's part of the horror of speaking, of writing. There is nowhere to hide. When you try to hide, the spectacle can grow grotesque. Think of Joan Didion's preemptive attempt, in *Blue Nights,* to quash any notion that her daughter Quintana Roo's childhood was a privileged one. "'Privilege' is a judgment. 'Privilege' is an opinion. 'Privilege' is an accusation. 'Privilege' remains an area to which—when I think of what [Quintana] endured, when I consider what came later—I will not easily cop." These remarks were a pity, since her account of "what came later"— Quintana's death, on the heels of the death of Didion's beloved husband—underscores Didion's more interesting, albeit disavowed subject, which is that economic privilege does not protect against all suffering.

I am interested in offering up my experience and performing my particular manner of thinking, for whatever they are worth. I would also like to cop easily to my abundant privilege—except that the notion of privilege as something to which one could "easily cop," as in "cop to once and be done with," is ridiculous. Privilege *saturates,* privilege *structures.* But I have also never been less interested in arguing for the rightness, much less the righteousness, of any particular position or orientation. *What* Deleuze/Parnet *other reason is there for writing than to be traitor to one's own*

*reign, traitor to one's own sex, to one's class, to one's majority? And
to be traitor to writing.*

Afraid of assertion. Always trying to get out of "totalizing" language, i.e., language that rides roughshod over specificity; realizing this is another form of paranoia. Barthes found the exit to
this merry-go-round by reminding himself that "it is language
which is assertive, not he." It is absurd, Barthes says, to try to
flee from language's assertive nature by "add[ing] to each sentence some little phrase of uncertainty, as if anything that came
out of language could make language tremble."

My writing is riddled with such tics of uncertainty. I have no
excuse or solution, save to allow myself the tremblings, then
go back in later and slash them out. In this way I edit myself
into a boldness that is neither native nor foreign to me.

At times I grow tired of this approach, and all its gendered baggage. Over the years I've had to train myself to wipe the *sorry* off
almost every work e-mail I write; otherwise, each might begin,
Sorry for the delay, Sorry for the confusion, Sorry for *whatever.*
Monique Wittig *One only has to read interviews with outstanding women to hear
them apologizing.* But I don't intend to denigrate the power of
apology: I keep in my *sorry* when I really mean it. And certainly
there are many speakers whom I'd like to see do more trem-
bling, more unknowing, more apologizing.

While beholding Steiner's *Puppies and Babies,* I couldn't help
but think of Nan Goldin's 1986 "visual diary," *The Ballad of
Sexual Dependency*—another series of photographs that bears
witness to the friends, lovers, and exes that make up the photog-

rapher's tribe. As the titles of the two works suggest, however, their moods differ sharply. One of the most Goldinesque photos in *Puppies and Babies* is an interior shot, just out of focus, of dancer Layla Childs (Steiner's ex), half-dressed and staring blankly at the camera, bathed in a dim red light. But instead of sporting a tear-stained face or bruises from a recent battering, à la *Ballad*, Childs is pumping milk from her breasts via a "hands free" pumping bra and double electric pump.

Pumping milk is, for many women, a sharply private activity. It can also be physically and emotionally challenging, as it reminds the nursing mother of her animal status: just another mammal, milk being siphoned from its glands. Beyond photographs in breast pump manuals (and lactation porn), however, images of milk expression are really nowhere to be found. Phrases such as *colostrum, letdown,* and *hindmilk* arrive in one's life like hieroglyphs from the land of the lost. So the presence of Steiner's camera here—and the steadfast stare of her subject—feels jarring and exciting. This is especially so when you consider how photographers such as Goldin (or Ryan McGinley, or Richard Billingham, or Larry Clark, or Peter Hujar, or Zoe Strauss) often make us feel as though we have glimpsed something radically intimate by evoking danger, suffering, illness, nihilism, or abjection. In Steiner's intimate portrait of Childs, the proposed transmission of fluids is about nourishment. *I almost can't imagine.*

And yet—while pumping milk may be about nourishment, it isn't really about communion. A human mother expresses milk because sometimes she can't be there to nurse her baby, either by choice or by necessity. Pumping is thus an admission of distance, of maternal finitude. But it is a separation, a finitude, suffused with best intentions. Milk or no milk, this is often the best we've got to give.

Once I suggested that I had written half a book drunk, the other half sober. Here I estimate that about nine-tenths of the words in this book were written "free," the other one-tenth, hooked up to a hospital-grade breast pump: words piled into one machine, milk siphoned out by another.

The phrase "toxic maternal" refers to a mother whose milk delivers poison along with nourishment. If you turn away from the poison, you also turn away from the nourishment. Given that human breast milk now contains literal poisons, from paint thinners to dry-cleaning fluid to toilet deodorizers to rocket fuel to DDT to flame retardants, there is literally no escape. Toxicity is now a question of degree, of acceptable parts per unit. Infants don't get to choose—they take what they can get, in their scramble to stay alive.

I had never thought much about this dilemma until after I had been working for many years in a bar that was regularly voted "a smoker's paradise" in a New York City guidebook. I had quit smoking a few months before taking the job, primarily because cigarettes made me feel so completely awful, and now I was spending hundreds, if not thousands, of dollars on an acupuncturist to help me with swollen glands and difficulty breathing as a result of inhaling smoke that wasn't even mine. (I ended up quitting the job about a month before Mayor Bloomberg's ban took effect; in my final hours, I secretly allowed myself to be interviewed by the antismoking crusaders, to advance their cause.) Anyone to whom I complained at the time said—wisely!—*Why don't you just get a different job? There are hundreds upon hundreds of restaurants and bars in New York City.* My therapist—I had taken on yet another choking shift in order to keep seeing her—suggested I help rich kids study for the SAT instead, which made me want to sock her. How could I explain? I had already had a hundred restaurant jobs in New York City, and finally I had found one at which I made more in a week than I would have in an entire semester as an adjunct instructor (the other discernible option). I also thought—a larval Karen Silkwood—*if "they"*—whoever *they* are—*let me work here, it couldn't be that bad, could it?*

But it was that bad. The bills I stashed under my mattress were almost wet with smoke, and stayed that way until rent time. And it's only now that I see that the job ensured me something else I needed: the constant company of alcoholics apparently worse off than I was. I can still see them all: the silent owner who had to be carried into the back of a taxi at dawn after he'd blacked out from Rolling Rocks and shots of Stoli that we'd served him, raking in his Wall Street–derived tips; the punk Swedes who drank shot after shot of jalapeno-pickled vodka dissolved in iced coffee (the Swedeball, we called it); the rotted teeth of a successful foley editor; the man who inexplicably took off his belt after a few Hurricanes and started whipping a fellow diner with it; the woman who left her baby in a car seat under the bar one night and forgot about it . . . their example, and the ease with which I deemed myself together by comparison, purchased me a few more years of believing alcohol more precious than toxic to me.

The self without sympathetic attachments is either a fiction or a lunatic. . . . [Yet] dependence is scorned even in intimate relationships, as though dependence were incompatible with self-reliance rather than the only thing that makes it possible.

Adam Phillips/
Barbara Taylor

I learned this scorn from my own mother; perhaps it laced my milk. I therefore have to be on the alert for a tendency to treat other people's needs as repulsive. Corollary habit: deriving the bulk of my self-worth from a feeling of hypercompetence, an irrational but fervent belief in my near total self-reliance.

You're a great student because you don't have any baggage, a teacher once told me, at which moment the subterfuge of my life felt complete.

One of the gifts of recognizing oneself in thrall to a substance is the perforation of such subterfuge. In place of an exhausting autonomy, there is the blunt admittance of dependence, and its subsequent relief. I will always aspire to contain my shit as best I can, but I am no longer interested in hiding my dependencies in an effort to appear superior to those who are more visibly undone or aching. Most people decide at some point that it

Butler

is *better . . . to be enthralled with what is impoverished or abusive than not to be enthralled at all and so to lose the condition of one's being and becoming.* I'm glad not to be there right now, but I'm also glad to have been there, to know how it is.

Sedgwick was a famous pluralizer, an instinctive maximalist who named and celebrated her predilection for profusion as "fat art." I celebrate this fat art, even if in practice I am more of a serial minimalist—an employee, however productive, of the condensery. Rather than a philosopher or a pluralizer, I may

Deleuze/Parnet

be more of an empiricist, insofar as my *aim is not to rediscover the eternal or the universal, but to find the conditions under which something new is produced* (creativeness).

I have never really thought of myself as a "creative person"— writing is my only talent, and writing has always felt more clarifying than creative to me. But in contemplating this definition, I wonder if one might be creative (or queer, or happy, or held) *in spite of* oneself.

That's enough. You can stop now: the phrase Sedgwick said she longed to hear whenever she was suffering. (Enough hurting, enough showing off, enough achieving, enough talking, enough trying, enough writing, enough living.)

The *capaciousness* of growing a baby. The way a baby literally *makes space* where there wasn't space before. The cartilage nub where my ribs used to fit together at the sternum. The little slide in my lower rib cage when I twist right or left that didn't used to slide. The rearrangement of internal organs, the upward squeezing of the lungs. The dirt that collects on your belly button when it finally pops inside out, revealing its bottom— finite, after all. The husky feeling in my postpartum perineum, the way my breasts filling all at once with milk is like an orgasm but more painful, powerful as a hard rain. While one nipple is getting sucked, the other sometimes sprays forth, unstoppable.

When I was writing on the poet James Schuyler in graduate school, my adviser noted in passing that I seemed oddly compelled by the idea of Schuyler's flaccidity. His comments on this account made me feel guilty, as if he thought I were trying to neuter or castrate Schuyler, a closet Solanas. I wasn't, at least not consciously. I just liked the way that Schuyler seemed to be performing, especially in his long poems, a drive to speech or creation not synonymous with desire in any typical sublimated-lust kind of a way. He had a cruising eye, to be sure (here he is in a grocery store: "I grabbed / a cart, went wheeling / up and down the aisles trying to get a front view of / him and see how he was / Hung and what his face was like"). But his poetics struck me as refreshingly without a will to power, or even a will to perversity. They feel triumphantly wilted, like so many of the flowers Schuyler paid tribute to.

This wiltedness may have had, in part, a chemical root. As Schuyler writes in "The Morning of the Poem": "Remember what / The doctor said: I am: remembering and staying / off [the sauce]: mostly it's not / So hard (indeed): did you know a side effect of / Antabuse can be to make / You impotent? Not that I need much help in that / department these days." The climactic expulsion at the poem's end is not come, but urine. Recalling a night long ago, drunk on Pernod in Paris, Schuyler writes: "I made it: there I was, confronting a urinal: I / inched down my zipper and put my right hand into / The opening: hideous trauma, there was just no way I could / transfer my swollen tool from hand to hand without a great / Gushing forth (inside my pants), like when Moses hit the rock: so / I did it: there was piss all over Paris, not to mention my shirt and pants, light sun tans."

"The Morning of the Poem" takes place, as do many of Schuyler's poems, against the backdrop of his mother's home in East Aurora, New York. As he moves in and out of memory and anecdote, his mother shuffles around the house, plays the radio all night, leaves out the dishes *just so,* watches her TV programs, jokes about the size of a skunk in the trash, and bickers with Schuyler about his desire to leave the windows open to the rain ("'*I'm* the one who will have to clean it up,'" she snarls, the maternal refrain). Schuyler's other great epic poem, "A Few Days," finishes his mother's story, ending with the lines: "Margaret Daisy Connor Schuyler Ridenour, / rest well, / the weary journey done."

It feels important to pause and pay homage to the fact that many of the many gendered-mothers of my heart—Schuyler, Ginsberg, Clifton, Sedgwick—are or were or have been corpulent beings. ("Whom do I mean when I say 'there's nothing wrong with us'?," asks poet Fred Moten. "The fat ones. The ones who are out of all compass however precisely they are located . . . My cousins. All my friends.") Or, as poet CAConrad writes: "Coming from white trash has advantages people with money don't seem to understand. For years, I've watched friends whose parents are doctors and bankers live in FEAR (even while rebelling) that they don't achieve enough, aren't good enough, clean enough, and especially NOT thin enough. . . . Now, if you don't mind I have a date with a delicious smartass with a trick jaw who's on his way over to my place with freshly made chocolate pudding and a can of whipped cream!"

And yet, at the same time, it feels disingenuous of me not to acknowledge that on a literal level, having a small body, a slender body, has long been related to my sense of self, even my sense of freedom.

This comes as no real surprise—my mother and her entire family line are obsessed with skinniness as an indicator of physical, moral, and economic fitness. My mother's skinny body, and her lifelong obsession with having *zero fat,* almost makes me disbelieve that she ever housed my sister or me inside of her. (I gained fifty-four pounds to grow an Iggy—a number that appalled my mother, and gave me the pleasure of a late-breaking disobedience.) One time my mother saw her shadow on a wall at a restaurant, and before she recognized it as hers, she said it looked like a skeleton. *Look how fat everyone is,* my mother says, her mouth agape, whenever we visit her ancestral Michigan. Her skinniness is proof that she moved up, got out.

A writer is someone who plays with the body of his mother. I am a writer; I must play with the body of my mother. Schuyler does it; Barthes does it; Conrad does it; Ginsberg does it. Why is it so hard for me to do it? For while I've come to know my own body as a mother, and while I can imagine the bodies of a multitude of strangers as my mother (basic Buddhist meditation), I still have a hard time imagining my mother's body as my mother.

I can easily conjure my father's body, though he has been dead thirty years. I can see him in the shower—tan, red, steaming, singing. I can conjure the slight oiliness of the curls on the back of his head, curls now present on Iggy. I can remember how certain clothes looked on him: a gray cable-knit sweater, his old Levi's, his daily suit. He was a density of heat and energy and joy and sexuality and song. I recognized him.

I think my mother is beautiful. But her negative feelings about her body can generate a force field that repels any appreciation of it. I've long known the drill: Boobs, too small. Butt, too big. Face, bird-like. Upper arms, old. But it's not just age—she even disparages the way she looks in baby pictures.

I don't know why she has never seen herself as beautiful. I think I've been waiting all these years for her to do so, as if that kind of self-love would somehow offer her body to me. But now I realize—she already gave it to me.

At times I imagine her in death, and I know that her body, in all its details, will flood me. I do not know how I will survive it.

I have always hated Hamlet—the character—for his misogynistic moping around after his mother's remarriage. And yet

I know I carry a kernel of Hamlet within me. In fact, I have proof: a childhood diary, in which I swore to one day exact revenge on my mother and stepfather for their affair, which broke up my parents' marriage. (My father's untimely death unfortunately occurred shortly thereafter.) I swore in my diary that my sister and I would stand forever with the ghost of our dead father, who now looked down upon us, betrayed and heartbroken, from heaven.

Also like Hamlet, I was angrier at my mother than at my stepfather, who was essentially a stranger. He had been the young housepainter in white pants who would sometimes stay late into the evening when my father was out of town on a business trip. On such nights, my sister and I would put on skits or dances for him and my mother: jesters for the queen and ersatz king. Not long after, he and my mother were walking down the aisle. When the reverend asked us to bend our heads in prayer, I kept my chin up, a sentinel.

For the duration of her marriage to my stepfather, my mother's maternal body seemed to me supplanted by her desiring body. For I knew that my stepfather wasn't just the object of her desire. I knew she believed him to *be* her desire, incarnate. Such thinking set her up for a bitter fall when he left her, twenty-odd years later, confessing all kinds of infidelities on his way out the door.

I hated him for crushing her. I hated her for being crushed.

When I was a teenager, my mother tried to explain her reasons for leaving my father in more adult terms. But even at thirteen I didn't know what to do with the notion that she needed to leave him "to have a chance at joy." My father seemed to me the vessel of all earthly joy; his death had but deepened this impression.

Why wasn't he good enough? *He told me that I could work out-side the home if I wanted to, so long as his shirts still got ironed and were ready for work the next day,* my mother told me. The feminist in me was unmoved. *Couldn't you have told him you didn't want to iron his shirts, and taken it from there?*

When my stepfather finally left, my sister and I felt as much relief as grief. The intruder had finally been expelled. The sodomitical mother would melt away, and the maternal body would be ours, at last.

No wonder, then, that our mother's announcement that she was getting married again caught us off guard, just a few years later. As she and her husband-to-be told us the news at a dinner party orchestrated, to our surprise, for just that purpose, I watched my sister turn a furious red, then lunge around for a vine that could hold her. *Well, if the wedding is in June, I'm not going,* she sputtered. *It's way too hot in June for anyone to get married. If it's in June I'm not going.* She was ruining the moment, and I loved her for it.

But this time, so far as I can tell, my mother has not made her husband her desire incarnate, though she does love him very much. And for his part, so far as I can tell, he doesn't try to talk her out of her self-deprecation, nor does he abet it. He simply loves her. I am learning from him.

About twenty-four hours after I gave birth to Iggy, the nice woman at the hospital who tested his hearing gave me a wide white elastic band for my postpartum belly, basically a giant Ace bandage with a Velcro waist. I was grateful for it, as my middle felt like it was about to slide off me and onto the floor.

Falling forever, falling to pieces. Maybe this belt would keep it, me, together. When she handed it to me, she winked and said, *Thanks for doing your part to keep America beautiful.*

I stumbled back to my hospital room, newly corseted, my gratitude now speckled with bewilderment. *What's my part? Having a baby? Taking measures to stop the spread? Not falling to pieces?*

It is unnerving, though, this melting. This pizza-dough-like flesh hanging down in folds where there used to be a pregnant tautness.

Don't think of it as, You've lost your body, one postpartum website counseled. *Think of it as, You gave your body to your baby.*

I gave my body to my baby. I gave my body to my baby. I'm not sure I want it back, or in what sense I could ever have it.

Throughout my postpartum delirium, I found myself lazily clicking on articles on my AOL home page (yes, AOL) about how certain celebrities got back into shape or into being sexual after babies. It's humdrum but relentless: the obsession with who's pregnant and who's showing and whose life is transforming due to the imminent arrival of the all-miraculous, all-coveted BABY—all of which flips, in the blink of an eye, into an obsession with how soon all signs of bearing the life-transforming BABY can evaporate, how soon the mother's career, sex life, weight can be restored, *as if nothing ever happened here at all.*

Who cares what SHE feels like doing? It's her conjugal duty to get over a massive physical event that has literally rearranged her organs and stretched her parts beyond comprehension and brought her through a life-or-death portal as soon as humanly possible. As in this post by a woman on Marriage Missions, a Christian website that hopes "to help those who are married and those preparing for marriage to be PRO-ACTIVE in helping to save marriage from divorce": "I felt what I did all day was meet other people's needs. Whether it was caring for my children, working in ministry, or washing my husband's clothes, by the end of the day I wanted to be done need-meeting. I wanted my pillow and a magazine. But God prompted me: 'Are the "needs" you meet for your husband the needs he wants met?'" The answer of course is NO! No less than GOD says she needs to put aside the sanity-producing magazine and pillow and start fucking her husband! Get over yourself and start fucking! God says, get GGG!

GGG: Good, Giving, and Game. That's sex-advice columnist Dan Savage's acronym, meaning "good in bed," "giving equal time and equal pleasure," and "game for anything—within reason." "If you are expected to be monogamous and have one person be all things sexually for you, then you have to be whores for each other," Savage says. "You have to be up for anything."

These are solid guidelines to which I have long aspired. But now I think we have a right to our kink and our fatigue, both.

In an age all too happy to collapse the sodomitical mother into the MILF, how can rampant, "deviant" sexual activity remain the marker of radicality? What sense does it make to align "queer" with "sexual deviance," when the ostensibly straight world is having no trouble keeping pace? Who, in the straight world, besides some diehard religious conservatives, truly experiences sexual pleasure as inextricably linked to reproductive function? Has anyone looked at the endless list of fetishes on a "straight" porn website recently? Have you read, as I did this morning, about the trial of Officer Gilberto Valle? If queerness is about disturbing normative sexual assumptions and practices, isn't one of these that sex is the be-all and end-all? What if Beatriz Preciado is right—what if we've entered a new, post-Fordist era of capitalism that Preciado calls the "pharmacopornographic era," whose principal economic resource is nothing other than "the insatiable bodies of the multitudes—their cocks, clitorises, anuses, hormones, and neurosexual synapses . . . [our] desire, excitement, sexuality, seduction, and . . . pleasure"?

Faced with the warp speed of this "new kind of hot, psycho-tropic, punk capitalism," especially from my station of fatigue, exchanging horniness for exhaustion grows in allure. Unable to fight my station, at least for the time being, I try to learn from it; another self, stripped.

Preciado

I first met Sedgwick in a graduate seminar titled Non-Oedipal Models of Psychology. By way of introduction, she announced that she had started going to therapy because she wanted to be happier. To hear a scary theoretical heavyweight admit such a thing changed my life. Then, without missing a beat, she said she wanted to play a quick get-to-know-you game involving totem animals.

Totem animals? How could it be that I had fled the spacey Haight-Ashbury of my youth for hard-core, intellectual New York, explicitly to escape games involving totem animals, only to find myself in the middle of one in a doctoral classroom? The game placed an icy finger on my identity phobia: it was but a short leap from here, I felt, to the index card, Sharpie, and lapel pin.

Perhaps anticipating this horror, Sedgwick explained to us that the game had a kind of out. She said that we were free to offer up a fake animal, a kind of decoy identification, if we so desired—if, for example, we had a "real" totem animal that we would prefer to keep to ourselves.

I didn't have a real or fake animal, and so I just sweated as we went around the room. When it got to me, I burped out *otter.* Which was a form of true. It was important to me back then to feel, to be wily. To feel small, slick, quick, amphibious, dexterous, capable. I didn't know then Barthes's book *The Neutral,* but if I had, it would have been my anthem—the Neutral being that which, in the face of dogmatism, the menacing pressure to take sides, offers novel responses: to flee, to escape, to demur, to shift or refuse terms, to disengage, to turn away. The otter was thus a complex sort of stand-in, or fake-out, another identity I felt sure I could shimmy out of.

But whatever I am, or have since become, I know now that slipperiness isn't all of it. I know now that a studied evasiveness has its own limitations, its own ways of inhibiting certain forms of happiness and pleasure. The pleasure of abiding. The pleasure of insistence, of persistence. The pleasure of obligation, the pleasure of dependency. The pleasures of ordinary devotion. The pleasure of recognizing that one may have to undergo the same realizations, write the same notes in the margin, return to the same themes in one's work, relearn the same emotional truths, write the same book over and over again— not because one is stupid or obstinate or incapable of change, but because such revisitations constitute a life.

"Many people doing all kinds of work are able to take pleasure in aspects of their work," Sedgwick once wrote, "but something different happens when the pleasure is not only taken but openly displayed. I like to make that different thing happen."

One happy thing that can happen, according to Sedgwick, is that pleasure becomes accretive as well as autotelic: the more it's felt and displayed, the more proliferative, the more possible, the more habitual, it becomes.

But, as Sedgwick knew well, there are other, more sinister models. A famous example from Sedgwick's own life makes this clear. In 1991, the year Sedgwick was first diagnosed with breast cancer, Sedgwick's essay "Jane Austen and the Masturbating Girl" was made notorious by right-wing culture warriors before Sedgwick had even written it. (They found the title in a Modern Language Association program and went to town from there.) About learning she was ill just as the "journalistic hologram bearing [her] name" became the object of ugly vitriol, she writes: "I don't know a gentler way to say it than that at a time when I've needed to make especially deep draughts on the reservoir of a desire to live and thrive, that resource has shown the cumulative effects of my culture's wasting depletion of it." She then names a few of the "thousand things [that] make it impossible to mistake the verdict on queer lives and on women's lives, as on the lives of those who are poor or are not white." This verdict can become a chorus of voices in our heads, standing by to inhibit our capacity to contend with illness, dread, and devaluation. "[These voices] speak to us," Sedgwick says. "They have an amazing clarity."

The way Sedgwick interprets it, it wasn't just her linking of a canonical writer with the filthy specter of self-pleasuring that struck her critics as depraved. More galling was the spectacle of a writer or thinker—be it Sedgwick or Austen—who finds her work happy-making, and who celebrates it publicly as such.

Worse still, in a culture committed to bleeding the humanities to death, along with any other labors of love that don't serve the God of capital: the spectacle of someone who likes her pointless, perverse work and gets paid—even paid well—for it.

Most writers I know nurse persistent fantasies about the horrible things—or *the* horrible thing—that will happen to them if and when they express themselves as they desire. (Everywhere I go as a writer—especially if I'm in drag as a "memoirist"—such fears seem to be first and foremost on people's minds. People seem hungry, above all else, for permission, and a guarantee against bad consequences. The first, I try to give; the second is beyond my power.) When I published my book *Jane: A Murder*—a book that took as its subject the 1969 murder of my mother's younger sister—I too nursed terrible fears: namely, that I would be murdered as Jane was, as punishment for my writerly transgressions. It took the writing of not only that book, but also an unintended sequel, for me to undo this knot, and hand its strands to the wind.

Now, this story is old news, especially for me. The reason I'm bringing it up again is that, in the months directly preceding Iggy's conception, I was interrupted for a spell by a stalker of sorts—a man obsessed with Jane's murder, and with me as someone who had written about it. It started with a message on my voice mail at work: a man called to say my aunt "got what she deserved," and called her a name. Specifically, he called her a "stupidhead." (Clearly "cunt" or "bitch" would have had its own spice, but "stupidhead," and the childish intonation in which it was delivered, generated its own species of alarm.)

I've worked in and around this subject long enough to know not to sit alone with such things, so I beelined down to the

Valencia sheriff's office, Harry by my side. The minute we opened the door, our spirits sank. The chubby white suburban teenagers impersonating cops were precisely the kind of men to whom we would have preferred *not* to unload this story. Nonetheless, I told the cop at the desk the briefest version I could manage, which spanned my aunt's 1969 murder to the writing of my two books to the voice mail left at my work that morning. He listened to me blankly, then pulled off a shelf a binder thick as a phone book, which he began pawing through at a glacial pace. After about five minutes, his face lit up. "Here it is," he said. *"Annoying phone call."* He proceeded to write out these three words in painstaking capital letters on a form. As he labored, another young cop ambled over. *What seems to be the problem here?* he said. I repeated the tale. He had me call my voice mail and play him the message, after which he looked up with theatrical indignation and said, "Now, what would someone go and say a thing like that for?"

I came home and hid the "annoying phone call" report in the back of a file drawer, and hoped that was that.

A few days later, after picking up my mail at work, I found a handwritten letter from one of my students in the mix. In it he said he was very sorry to intrude upon my day, but he wanted me to know that a strange man was on campus looking for me. He said the man was stopping people in the cafeteria, in the library, at the security gate, asking if they knew me, and talking obsessively about my aunt's murder, saying he needed to deliver me an important message. My dean got wind of the situation and whisked me into her office, where I stayed for the next four hours with the doors locked and the blinds drawn while waiting for the police to arrive—an experience that is fast becoming a staple of the American educational scene rather than a disruption of it. After campus security interviewed the student who left me the letter, along with a host of other people on campus with whom the man had spoken, I was left with this description: "a balding, heavyset white man in his early fifties, carrying an attaché case."

Within forty-eight hours of his visit, as if acting out cinematic shorthand for how to deal with an unexpected, intense stress, I started smoking again—this after over two years of treating my body as a prenatal temple, my vices reduced to a single cup of green tea each morning. Now I sat in the backyard of our new house, a square clump of prickly weeds we felt unable to attend to until we knew how much money the pregnancy adventure was going to cost, inhaling egg-shriveling nicotine in the dark, a cylinder of pepper spray by my side. Other moments of my life may have looked worse, but this one felt like its own kind of bottom: I'd never felt so scared and nihilistic at the same time. I wept for the baby and the life I felt sure would never be ours, no matter how badly I wanted it, and for the violence that the stalker's presence seemingly confirmed as impossible to outrun.

In the days and weeks that followed, I summoned the strength to call our donor and tell him we'd be skipping the month, and to begin the struggle of hoisting myself back onto the prenatal regime. I tried to return to reflecting on happy-making things, including a happy-making talk about Sedgwick I was due to deliver at my happy-making alma mater, the City University of New York. But the mantras of paranoid thinking—*There must be no bad surprises* and *You can never be paranoid enough*—had taken root. I couldn't wait around for some wacko to "deliver me a message"; somehow I needed to get ahead of the situation.

It's hard to explain, but I have a lot of friends who are private investigators. One of them gave me the number of a local PI,

a guy named Andy Lamprey, described on a "total security so-
lutions provider" website as follows: "A detective for the Los
Angeles Police Department for more than 29 years, Lamprey
investigated numerous crimes, including homicide, and was
a senior supervisor to the Special Weapons and Tactics Team
(SWAT). He is a court qualified expert in narcotics and vice
enforcement and has performed several risk and vulnerability
assessments, threat and management assessments and fraud investigations nationwide."

You never know—there may come a time when you, too, feel
the need to call upon an Andy Lamprey.

Lamprey eventually connects me with a guy named Malcolm,
another ex-LAPD cop, who will sit, armed, in an unmarked
car outside our house through the night, keeping watch over
us, if we want. We want. Lamprey says he can negotiate us
a reduced rate of $500 per night (LA has unbelievably high
rates for "cover," as I learn it's called). I call my mother to ask
for advice, and also to alert her to the wingnut on the loose,
in case he drifts her way; she insists on putting a check in the
mail to pay for a night or two of Malcolm. I feel grateful, but
also guilty: it was I who had insisted on writing about Jane's
murder, and while I knew intellectually that I wasn't responsible for this man's actions any more than Jane was for her
murder (as the caller had indicated), my less enlightened self
felt sick with a sense of late-breaking comeuppance. I had summoned the horrible thing, and now here he was, attaché case
in hand. It wasn't long before my image of him merged with
that of Jared Lee Loughner, the man who, exactly two weeks
prior, had walked up to Representative Gabby Giffords in a
Safeway parking lot in Tucson, Arizona, and shot her, along
with eighteen others. A form letter from Giffords was found in
Loughner's home with the words "Die, Bitch" scrawled on it;

Loughner was known for saying that women should not hold positions of power.

It doesn't matter to me if both of these men are mad. Their voices still have clarity.

In the wake of the Patriot Act, during the second administration of George W., you made a series of small, handheld weapons. The rule was that each weapon had to be assembled from household items within minutes. You'd been gay-bashed before, two black eyes while waiting in line for a burrito (you ran after him, of course). Now you thought, if the government comes for its citizens, we should be prepared, even if our weapons are pathetic. Your art-weapons included a steak knife affixed to a bottle of ranch dressing and mounted on an axe handle, a dirty sock sprouting nails, a wooden stump with a clump of urethane resin stuck to one end with dull bolts protruding from it, and more.

One night during our courtship, I came home to find the stump with bolts lying across the welcome mat of my porch. You had left town, and I had been baffled by your departure. But when I ascended my front steps and saw the weapon, shadowy in the twilight, I knew you loved me. It was a talisman of protection—a means of keeping myself safe while you were gone, a tool to fight off the suitors (had there been any). I've kept it by my bedside ever since. Not because I think they're coming for us per se. But because it makes the brutal tender, which I've since learned is one of your principal gifts.

The year my father died, I read a story in school about a little boy who builds ships in the bottoms of bottles. This little boy lived by the maxim that if you could imagine the worst thing that could ever happen, you would never be surprised when it did. Not knowing that this maxim was the very definition of anxiety, as given by Freud ("'Anxiety' describes a particular state of expecting the danger or preparing for it, even though it may be an unknown one"), I set to work cultivating it. Already an avid "journaler," I started penning narratives of horrible things in my school notebook. My first installment was a novella titled "Kidnapped" that featured the abduction and torture of my best friend, Jeanne, and me by a deranged husband-wife team. I was proud of my talismanic opus, even drew an ornate cover page for it. Now Jeanne and I would never be kidnapped and tortured without our having foreseen it! I thus felt confused and saddened when my mother took me out for lunch "to talk about it." She told me she was disturbed by what I had written, and so was my sixth-grade teacher. In a flash it became clear that my story was not something to be proud of, as either literature or prophylactic.

When Iggy first came home from the hospital, in that ecstatic, disarranged week of almost no sleep, my intense happiness was sometimes punctured in the dead of night by the image of him with a half scissor sticking out of his precious newborn head. Perhaps I had put it there, or perhaps he had slipped and fallen into it. For whatever reason, this image seemed the very worst thing I could imagine. It came to me when I was trying to fall asleep, after many hours—sometimes many nights—of not sleeping. We were up so often that we put a red lightbulb in the living room lamp and kept it on all the time, so that there were periods of sun followed by periods of red, no real night. Once, while wandering in the red soup, I told Harry I was worried I was having a postpartum crash, as I was having bad thoughts about the baby. I couldn't tell him about the half scissor.

I can't remember now the connection between the little boy's building of ships in the bottles (*Argo*'s?) and his commitment to paranoid anxiety, but I'm sure there was one. Nor can I find the original story. I wish that I could find it, as I'm pretty sure its moral wasn't that all good comes from repeatedly imagining the worst things that could ever happen. Likely a wise old crinkly grandpa drifts into the tale and disabuses his grandson of his rotten notion by taking him to see some wild birds flying over a hillside. But now I think I'm mixing and matching.

That wise old crinkly grandparent has not yet waltzed into my life. Instead I have my mother, who lives and breathes the gospel of prophylactic anxiety. When I tell her that it would be easier for me if she could keep her anxieties about my newborn to herself, rather than have her e-mail me to tell me that she's having trouble sleeping for fear of bad things happening to him (and to everyone else she loves), she snaps: "They're not all irrational anxieties, you know."

My mother thinks that people don't really know what they're in for in this life—what the *risks* are. How could there be such a thing as an irrational peril, if anything unexpected or horrific that has ever happened could happen again? Last February a sinkhole opened up under a man's bedroom near Tampa, Florida, while he was sleeping; his body will never be found. When Iggy was six months old, he was stricken by a potentially fatal nerve toxin that afflicts about 150 babies of the 4 million+ born in the United States each year.

Recently my mother visited the Killing Fields in Cambodia. After she returned, she sat in our living room showing me her trip photos while Iggy motored around the shaggy white rug, doing "tummy time." *I barely want to tell you about this, because of the baby,* she said, nodding in his direction, *but there was a tree there, an oak tree, called the Killing Tree, against which the Khmer Rouge would kill babies by bashing their skulls. Thousands and thousands of babies, their brains smashed out against this tree.* I get the point, I say. *I'm sorry,* she says, *I really shouldn't be telling you this.*

A few weeks later, talking about her trip again on the phone, she says, *Now, there's something I shouldn't really mention, because of the baby, but they had this tree there, at the Killing Fields, called the Killing Tree . . .*

I know my mother well enough by now to recognize, in her baby-killing-tree Tourette's, her desire to install in me an outer parameter of horror of what could happen to a baby human on this planet. I don't know why she needs to feel sure I have this parameter in mind, but I have come to accept that she feels it necessary. She needs me to know that she's stood before the Killing Tree.

For the week after the man's visit to my work, campus security will assign an officer to stand outside the door of my classroom while I teach, in case he returns. On one of these days, I teach Alice Notley's grouchy epic poem *Disobedience.* A student complains, *Notley says she wants a dailiness that is free and beautiful, but she's fixated on all the things she hates and fears the most, and then smashes her face and ours in them for four hundred pages. Why bother?*

Empirically speaking, we are made of star stuff. Why aren't we talking more about that? Materials never leave this world. They just keep recycling, recombining. That's what you kept telling me when we first met—that in a real, material sense, *what* is made from *where.* I didn't have a clue what you were talking about, but I could see you burned for it. I wanted to be near that burning. I still don't understand, but at least now my fingers ride the lip.

Notley knows all this; it's what tears her up. It's why she's a mystic, why she locks herself in a dark closet, why she knocks herself out to have visions. Can she help it if the unconscious is a sewer? At least my student had unwittingly backed us into a crucial paradox, which helps to explain the work of any number of artists: *it is sometimes the most paranoid-tending people who are able to, and need to, develop and disseminate the richest reparative practices.*

In Annie Sprinkle's performance piece *100 Blow Jobs,* Sprinkle—who worked for many years as a prostitute—kneels down on the ground and gives head to several dildos nailed to a board in front of her, while recorded male voices yell degrading things like "Suck it, bitch." (Sprinkle has said that out of the approximately 3,500 customers she had as a sex worker, there were about 100 bad ones; the sound track to *100 Blow Jobs* derives from the bad ones.) She sucks and sucks, she chokes and gags. But just when someone might be thinking, *This is exactly what I imagined sex work to be like—haunting, woman-hating, traumatizing*—Sprinkle gets up, pulls herself together, gives herself an Aphrodite Award for sexual service to the community, and performs a cleansing masturbatory ritual.

Sprinkle is a many-gendered mother of the heart. And many-gendered mothers of the heart say: *Just because you have enemies does not mean you have to be paranoid.* They insist, no matter the evidence marshaled against their insistence: *There is noth-*

ing you can throw at me that I cannot metabolize, no thing impervious to my alchemy.

The realization that I could incorporate the stalker into my talk about Sedgwick eventually became an incitement for me to get back to work. *Yes, get back to work.* It even became a source of comfort, as if bringing such an episode into the orbit of Eve would neutralize its negative force.

Not everyone believes in the magical powers of such an approach. When I told my mother that I was thinking of including the stalker in a public talk, for example, she said, "Oh honey, are you sure that's a good idea?"—meaning that she didn't think it was a good idea at all. Who could blame her? She's spent over forty years warding off the specter of wingnuts with attaché cases who tell women they deserve their violent deaths before they occasion them. Why give them any more attention than they deserve?

Most of my writing usually feels to me like a bad idea, which makes it hard for me to know which ideas feel bad because they have merit, and which ones feel bad because they don't. Often I watch myself gravitating toward the bad idea, as if the final girl in a horror movie, albeit one sitting in a Tuff Shed at a desk sticky with milk. But somewhere along the line, from my heroes, whose souls were forged in fires infinitely hotter than mine, I gained an outsized faith in articulation itself as its own form of protection.

I am not going to write anything here about Iggy's time with the toxin; it is not precious or rich to me. All I will say is that there is still a loop of time, or there is still a part of me, that is removing the side of a raised hospital crib in the morning light and climbing into it beside him, unwilling to move or let go or keep living until he lifted his head, until he gave any sign that he would make it out.

The bummer about stalkers, Lamprey told me when we first spoke, is that the best thing that can happen is nothing. *You don't really want any form of contact that would merit a court date or a call to 911,* he said. *You just want the days of silence to add up.*

By the third night of Malcolm's watch, I started having delusions that he could sit outside our house forever, to protect against whatever. But the money had run out, as had the logic of the enterprise. We were on our own.

The task of the cervix is to stay closed, to make an impenetrable wall protecting the fetus, for approximately forty weeks of a pregnancy. After that, by means of labor, the wall must somehow become an opening. This happens through dilation, which is not a shattering, but an extreme thinning. *(O so thin!)*

This feeling has its ontological merits, but it is not really a good feeling. It's easy enough to stand on the outside and say, "You just have to let go and let the baby out." But to let the baby out, you have to be willing to go to pieces.

Thirty-nine weeks. I take a long walk across the campus of Occidental College. It's a hair too hot, as it always is in Los Angeles, where the sun has no mercy. I come home frustrated, taut with baby, anxious for it. Harry has friends over; they are getting ready for a movie shoot, wearing dingy white outfits and hats with skinny white ceramic horns that Harry inexplicably asserts make them look like lice. *Don't let the lice talk to me,* I say, pulling down the shades. I feel feral, a little sad, very full. Backache.

The previous day, walking in the arroyo, green and fresh, I had invited the baby out. *Time to rumble, Iggy.* I knew he heard me.

Some pains start. The lice go home. For no good reason we decide to rearrange the bookshelves. We'd been meaning to do it for weeks, and Harry suddenly feels frantic to get it done, make things right. I keep sitting down to rest amid the books on the floor, arranging them into piles by genre, then by country. More pains. All these beautiful pages.

Harry calls Jessica, says, Come now. Tried to sleep, but the night began to cavern. New dim lights in the house, new sounds. Birds chirping in the middle of the night while I labor in the tub. Jessica asks if the birds are real. They are. She rigs our tub with duct tape and a plastic bag so the tub can grow big with water. She has tricks. I keep wondering bleakly why she's texting through my labor; later I learn she has an app on her iPhone that times the contractions. Night passes quickly, in the time that is no time.

In the morning Harry and Jessica persuade me to go for an hour walk, briskly, in the gray day. It's hard. *The contractions aren't going to stop if you stop moving,* Jessica keeps telling me. OK but how does she know. We walk down to the Rite Aid at York and Figueroa to get castor oil, but when we get there, no one has a wallet. I squint in the gray light. I am going, almost gone. Back to the house for wallets, back to the store, we pace the parking lot, which looks scabrous with trash. I want to be somewhere more beautiful, I think, and also, everything is right.

At home I eat the castor oil mixed into chocolate ice cream. I want what's inside to come out.

We'd been living together for just over a year when your mother received her diagnosis. She had gone to the doctor for back pain and was there told that she had breast cancer that had already spread to her spine, a tumor threatening to crack her vertebrae. Within months the cancer would reach her liver; within the year, her brain. We flew her out from Michigan when she became bedridden from radiation with no one to help. We gave her our bed, and started sleeping on our living room floor. We lived this way for months, all of us staring in dread and paralysis out at our mountain. We each anguished differently and severely: you wanted to give her the care she'd once given to you, but could see it was breaking our new household to try; she was sick and broke and terrified, utterly unwilling or unable to discuss her condition or her options. Eventually I, villainous, drew a line; I couldn't live this way. She chose to go back to her condo in the suburbs of Detroit and decline alone rather than accept the substandard care of a Medicaid facility near us— all her assets liquidated, a TV blaring from behind a neighbor's canvas curtain, nurses whispering about accepting Christ as your personal savior, you know the place. Who could blame her? She wanted to be at home, crowded in with her beloved Parisian-themed knickknacks—all her I LOVE PARIS plaques, miniature Eiffel Towers. All of her passwords and e-mail addresses were variants on Paris, a city she would never see.

As her time grew near, your brother took her in. His family situation was under strain, but at least she had a bed there, her own room. It was almost good enough.

But really none of it was good enough, even though it was better than many get. When she began to lose consciousness, your brother had her moved to a local hospice; you flew there in the dead of night, desperate to get there in time, so that she wouldn't die alone.

Now I'm sick of these two clowns who aren't in pain. I say I want to go to the hospital because that's where they take the babies out. Jessica stalls; she knows it's not time. I begin to get desperate. I want a change of scenery. I'm not sure I can do this. We've spent hours on the red couch with a heating pad, in the tub kneeling on towels, in the bed with me holding Harry's or Jessica's hand. I have to think of something that will convince them that it's time to go to the hospital. "The baby feels low, and I'm having it at the hospital, and that's where I want to be," I growl. Finally they say OK.

The car is where the pain turns into a luge. I can't open my eyes. Have to go inside. Outside there is a lot of traffic; I squint and see Harry doing the best he can. Every bump and turn a nightmare. The pain cavern has a law, its law is black shudder. I begin to count, noticing each one takes about twenty seconds. I think, any kind of pain must be bearable for twenty seconds, for nineteen, for thirteen, for six. I stop making sounds. It is horrible.

Hard time parking, no one around, even though every other time we've been to the labor wing there has been a bevy of attendants with wheelchairs. I am going to have to walk. I walk as slowly as a person could walk, doubled over down the hall. Jessica greets some people she knows. Everything around me is normal and inside I am in the pain cavern.

We check into the labor wing. The nurse is nice. Freckled, heavy-set, Irish-seeming. She says five centimeters. People are happy, I am happy. Jessica tells me the hard part is over, she says getting to five centimeters is the hard part. I am nervous but relieved. Jessica asks for room number 7. The hospital is blessedly slow, quiet, empty.

Room number 7 is lovely, dark. We can see Macy's from the window. Whitney Houston has just been found dead in a hotel about ten blocks away, the Beverly Hilton. The nurses are talking about it in hushed tones as they come and go. Was it drugs, I manage to ask from the cavern. Probably, they say. In our labor room there is a bathtub, a scale, and a baby warmer. Maybe there will be a baby.

The pain luge continues, the counting, the dedication, the quiet, the panic. I am phobic about the toilet. Jessica keeps wanting me to go pee, but sitting down or squatting is unthinkable. She keeps telling me I can't stop the contractions by staying immobile, but I think I can. I lie on my side, I squeeze Harry's or Jessica's hand. I pee without meaning to in a slow-dancing position with Harry, then in the tub, where strands of dark red mucus have started to float. Incredibly, Harry and Jessica order food and eat it. Someone feeds me a red Popsicle, which tastes delicious. I throw it up moments later, fouling my tub's waters. I throw up when the contraction hits bottom, over and over, tons of yellow bile.

The tub has a jets button we keep hitting accidentally, which is horrible. Jessica pours water over my body, which feels good.

They measure again: seven. That is good.

Hours later, they measure again. Still seven. Not so good.

We talk. They tell me the contractions are slowing down, getting less powerful. This could go on for hours. They say maybe five more hours, or more, to get to ten centimeters. I don't want that. It has been twenty-four hours of labor, maybe a little more. We talk Pitocin. The midwife says I have to be ready to get a lot more uncomfortable than I am now. I am scared. How deep can pain go.

But I want something to change. I want to do the drug. We do it. The pic line keeps getting bent, a small red alarm goes off each time, I am frustrated, the nurse keeps having to redo it. Twenty minutes go by. Then twenty more. They up the dosage once, then again. Turn into the new cavern, a cartoon turn. I grow very quiet and concentrated. Counting, counting. Jessica says breathe into the bottom and I can tell that's where the baby is.

each of the volunteers told me that my job was to let my mom know that it was ok to go. i believe that i was unconvincing for the first 33 hours of my time with her.

however on the last night, i put a pillow under her knees, and i told her i was going to take a walk. that i would smell honeysuckle

Harry

and see fireflies, wet my shoes in midnight dew. i told her that i was going to do those things because i was going to stay on earth in this form. "but your work here is done mama." i told her that she had set us all up very well with her love and her lessons. i told her she had inspired me to become an artist. i told her that i loved her so much, that we all knew that she loved us too, that she was surrounded in love, surrounded in light. and i walked. after my walk, among other things, i told her i was going to go to sleep, and she should too. i said it firmly. i told her to not be afraid, to relax, that it was ok if she had to go. i told her i knew she was tired and that all accounts of heaven (from those who have so briefly visited) are that it is pure bliss. i told her not to be afraid. i thanked her. i said, "thank you mom." i leaked tears but tried to hide them from her now. i turned on the bathroom light and closed the door so a long foot thick rectangle of yellow reached her from feet to head. i touched her feet over the blanket, then her thighs, her torso and bare chest below her throat, her shoulders her face and ears. i kissed her all over her beautiful bald head and i said, "goodnight mama. you go to sleep." and then i laid down in my little chair bed there put my jacket over my upper body and silently cried myself to sleep. the sound of her breathing, deep and gulping and certain.

It's very dark now. Harry and Jessica have fallen asleep. I am alone with the baby. I try to commit to the idea of letting him out. I still can't imagine it. But the pain keeps going deeper.

At the bottom, which one can't quite know is the bottom, one reckons. I've heard a lot of women describe this reckoning (it might also be called nine centimeters), at which one starts bargaining hard, as if striking a deal to save your conjoined lives. *I don't know how we're going to get out of this, baby, but word is that you've got to come out, and that I've got to let you, and we've got to do this together, and we've got to do it now.*

They tell me the baby is facing a weird way, I have to lie on my left side, with my leg elevated. I don't want to. They tell me twenty minutes this way. I see a collection of hands holding my leg. It hurts. After twenty minutes, he has turned.

They measure again. Fully effaced, fully dilated. The midwife is ecstatic. Says we're ready to go. I want to know what will happen next. Just wait, they say.

at a certain point i woke up. i listened for her breath, which i Harry
heard after a moment. much shallower, faster. i became alert, just then the AC unit went on, aurally overtaking the sound of her. this had happened innumerable times before, and it was always a strange bardo for me. would the breath still be happening when the fan went back off? i strained to hear her breath over the grinding of the fan but couldn't. my torso leapt and sat up to check if her chest was moving. it didn't seem to be. the AC roared. her left hand puffed the sheet up suddenly, the tiniest, instant halloween ghost. her first movement—a signaling. i leapt to her, to that hand. her eyes were open now, illuminated, looking up, her mouth was now closed, her face no longer tilted, akimbo. she was beautiful. and dying. her mouth was in slow-motion rounding up little bits of earth air for her lungs, or just an echo of that i guess. her eyes were in light and open. she was jutting her chin in the sweetest, most dignified little coquettish juts. she was in the doorway of all worlds and i was in the doorway too. i forced myself not to disturb her, she seemed all at once to know where she was going and how to get there. her map. her job. the goal at hand. i cupped her warm hand in mine and let her go. i told her one more time, you are surrounded in love, you are surrounded in light, don't be afraid. and her neck was pulsing a little bit? her eyes were looking at something in another place. her mouth needed less air, less often and her chin moving more slowly. i never wanted it to end. i have never wanted

infinity to open up under an instant like i wanted that then. and then her eyes relaxed and her shoulders relaxed of a piece. and i knew she had found her way. dared. summoned up her smarts and courage and whacked a way through. i was really astonished. proud of her. i looked at the clock it was 2:16.

They think my bladder is too full, that it's in the way. I can't stand up to pee anymore in the slow-dancing position. They put in a catheter. It stings. Then the doctor comes in, says he'd like to break the water, says it's enormously full. OK but how. He brandishes what appears to be a bamboo back scratcher. OK. The waters are broken. It feels tremendously good. I am lying in a warm ocean.

Suddenly, the urge to push. Everyone is thrilled. Push, they say. They teach me. Hold it in, hold in the air, bear down wildly, don't waste the end of the push. The midwife puts her hand in to see if I need help pushing. She says I am a good pusher and don't need any help. I am happy I am a good pusher. I want to try.

On the fourth or so contraction, he starts to come. I don't know for sure if it's him, but I can feel the change. I push hard. One push turns into another kind of push—I feel it outside.

Commotion. I am gone but happy, something is happening. The doctor rushes in, I can see him throwing on his gear: a visor, an apron. He seems agitated but who cares. New lights come on, yellow, directed lights. People around me are moving quickly. My baby is being born.

Everyone is watching down there intently, in a kind of happy panic. Someone asks if I want to feel the baby's head, and I don't, I don't know why. Then a minute later, I do. Here he comes. It feels big but I feel big enough.

Then suddenly they tell me to stop pushing. I don't know why. Harry tells me that the doctor is stretching my perineum in circles around the baby's head, trying to keep the skin from tearing. Hold, they say, don't push, but "puff." Puff puff puff.

Then they say I can push. I push. I feel him come out, all of him, all at once. I also feel the shit that had been bedeviling me all through pregnancy and labor come out too. My first feeling is that I could run a thousand miles, I feel amazing, total and complete relief, like everything that was wrong is now right.

And then, suddenly, Iggy. Here he comes onto me, rising. He is perfect, he is right. I notice he has my mouth, incredible. He is my gentle friend. He is on me, screaming.

Push again, they say a few moments later. *You've got to be kidding—aren't I done yet?* But this one's easy; the placenta has no bones. I had always imagined the placenta like a rare fifteen-ounce steak. Instead it's utterly indecent and colossal—a bloody yellow sac filled with purple-black organs, a bag of whale hearts. Harry stretches its hood and photographs its insides, awed by this most mysterious and gory of apartments.

When his first son was born, Harry cried. Now he holds Iggy close, laughing sweetly into his little face. I look at the clock; it is 3:45 A.M.

I spent another 5 hours with her body, alone, with the light on. she Harry *was so incredibly beautiful. she looked 19. i took about a hundred*

*pictures of her. i sat with her for a long long time holding her hand.
i prepared a meal and ate in the other room and returned. i kept
talking to her. i felt like i lived a hundred years, a lifetime with
her silent, peaceful body. i turned off the AC unit. the ceiling fan
above her was whipping air, holding the space of cycle, where her
breath had been. i could've stayed another hundred years right
there—kissing her and visiting with her. it would have been fine
with me. important.*

You don't do *labor,* I was counseled several times before the baby
came. *Labor does you.*

This sounded good—I like physical experiences that involve
surrender. I didn't know, however, very much about experiences that *demand* surrender—that run over you like a truck,
with no safe word to stop it. I was ready to scream, but labor
turned out to be the quietest experience of my life.

If all goes well, the baby will make it out alive, and so will you.
Nonetheless, you will have touched death along the way. You
will have realized that death will do you too, without fail and
without mercy. It will do you even if you don't believe it will
do you, and it will do you in its own way. There's never been a
human that it didn't. *I guess I'm just waiting to die,* your mother
said, bemused and incredulous, the last time we saw her, her
skin so thin in her borrowed bed.

People say women forget about the pain of labor, due to some
kind of God-given amnesia that keeps the species reproducing.
But that isn't quite right—after all, what does it mean for pain
to be "memorable"? You're either in pain or you're not. And it
isn't the pain that one forgets. It's the touching death part.

As the baby might say to its mother, we might say to death: *I forget you, but you remember me.*

I wonder if I'll recognize it, when I see it again.

We wanted a longer name for Iggy, but Ignatius seemed too Catholic, and other "Ign" names too-close cognates of undesirable concepts (*ignorant, ignoble*). Then one day I stumbled upon Igasho, a Native American name, meaning "he who wanders," tribe unknown. That's it, I instantly thought. To my surprise, you concurred. And so Iggy became Igasho.

The spectacle of two white Americans choosing a Native American name made me uneasy. But I remembered that, when we first met, you told me you were part Cherokee. This fact buoyed me along. When I mentioned this to you in the hospital, as we were filling out Iggy's birth certificate, you looked at me like I was crazy. *Part Cherokee?*

A few hours later, a lactation consultant came to visit us. She talked to us for a long time, told us all about her family. She was a member of the Pima tribe from Arizona and had married into an African American family, raised her six kids in Watts. She nursed them all. One of her sons was named Eagle Feather, Eagle for short. Her mother had insisted on a ceremony at which Eagle learned to say his name in his tribal language, as Eagle was the white man's language. *I don't know why I'm telling you guys so much about my family,* she kept saying. You were probably passing, but I like to think she had an intuition that something about identity was loose and hot in our house, as, perhaps, it was in hers. At some point we told her about wanting to name Igasho Igasho. She listened, while giving me tips on how to nurse him. *Let your boobs be the guide, not the clock,* she said. *Whenever they feel full, bam!, you pull that baby onto your chest.* On her way out, she turned and said, *If anyone ever gives you trouble about your baby's name, you tell them that a full tribe member, from Tucson and Watts, gave you her blessing.*

Later I learn that Pima was the name given to the Othama tribe by the Spaniards. It is a corruption, or misunderstanding, of the phrase *pi 'añi mac* or *pi mac,* meaning "I don't know"—a phrase tribe members supposedly said often in response to the invading Europeans.

A few months after your mother died, we got all her papers in the mail. One afternoon I sat on a milk crate outside our storage shed to give them a cursory look, trying to decide where to file them. Amid the mountains of medical bills and threatening collections statements, a certain set of papers stood out—papers with smiley faces and flowery mastheads, exclamation points and carefully handwritten signatures. Your adoption paperwork.

When you were born, you were Wendy Malone. Perhaps you were Wendy Malone for but minutes, or hours. We don't know. Your adoption had been arranged prior to your birth, and at three weeks old, you were delivered to your parents, whereupon you became Rebecca Priscilla Bard. Which is who you were for the next twenty-odd years. Becky. In college, you made a loose stab at renaming yourself Butch, though, hilariously, you didn't really know what it meant. It had just been a nickname for you, used by your father. After you knew, you could tell who was gay by introducing yourself. "I'm Butch," you'd say, swinging your long blond hair. "No you're not," those in the know would chuckle. Then, after dropping out of college and moving to San Francisco, in a Judy Chicago–style rebirth, you renamed yourself Harriet Dodge. After you had a child, you inched toward the state and made the change official: you placed an ad in the paper, filed the paperwork at the courthouse. (Until then, you'd kept your distance from "affairs of the state": no one had your correct Social Security number until you were thirty-six; you'd never had a bank account.) Over time you became Harriet "Harry" Dodge: an attempt to conjure the feeling of *and*, or *but*. Now you are simply Harry, the Harriet a distasteful but sometimes indicative appendage.

When the *New York Times* ran a piece on your art in 2008, the editor said you couldn't appear in their pages unless you chose *Mr.* or *Ms.* You'd been waiting your whole life for this kind of recognition; now here it was, but with this price. (You chose *Ms.*, "to take one for the team.") Around the same time, your ex wouldn't agree to a custody deal if you checked the box on the second-parent adoption forms that said "mother," but you couldn't by law check the box that said "father." (I judged you then for not having adopted your first son at birth, which would have obviated this torturous second-parent adoption process; to my surprise, I find that now I, too, am unwilling to undertake such a proceeding, vis-à-vis Iggy—I'd rather gamble on national LGBT legal momentum and the relatively progressive state of California than pay $10,000 in legal fees and allow a social worker into our home to interview our children, to deem us "fit.") When we visited your mother in the hospital, she would sometimes say how glad she was that her daughter was there with her; the nurses would then wheel around the room, looking for her. When we take Iggy to the doctor together now, the nurse always says how happy it makes her to see a father helping out with a baby. *I'm certainly doing their team a lot of favors,* you mutter. Conversely, there's at least one restaurant we don't go to anymore because the waiter had a Tourette's-like addiction to calling everyone in our family "ladies" every time he so much as deposited a bottle of catsup at our table. *He thinks we're all girls,* my stepson would whisper to us in bemusement. *That's OK—girls are very, very cool,* you would tell him. *I know,* he would say back.

In your early thirties, you went on a hunt for your birth mother. You didn't have much to go on, but eventually you found her: she was a newly sober leather dyke—quick, articulate, tough around the edges. One of the first things she told you was that she had worked as a prostitute in Nevada. You offered her some probable excuses; she cut you right off, saying she liked the work, and *if you got it, use it.* During your first phone conversation, you asked about your birth father; she sighed, "Oh honey, I'm just not sure." But when you met her for lunch at a Chili's, upon seeing you approach, she exclaimed, "It was Jerry!" She said you looked just like her other child, whose father was Jerry. She had frosty gray hair and wire spectacles, wore lipstick and wide-bottom linen pants. She told you her father (your natal grandfather) had just died and left her a little money, with which she was fixing up a craftsman in San Jose with her on-again, off-again butch lover.

All she told you then about Jerry was that he was "not a nice person." Later she said he was violent. She said she wasn't in touch with him anymore—the last she'd heard was that he was living on an island off Canada with holes cut out of the armpits of his shirt, to air out his shingles. A few years later, she told you he had died. You never wanted to know more.

Your birth brother, who was raised by his father, has long been an addict—in and out of prison, on and off the streets. He wrote you once from prison, in a style that uncannily echoed your own—the same careening prose, shot through with a meticulousness, a darkness, a hilarity. The last time she heard from him, your birth mother tells us, he had been found unconscious in a parking lot, covered in blood. Once he came to, he called her collect; she didn't accept the charge. She threw up her hands as she told us this story, saying, *I didn't have the money!* But we also heard her saying, *I can't carry him anymore.*

You had your last drink at twenty-three. You already knew.

It can be hard not to know much about one's parents. But, you tell me, it can be awesome too. Before you had thought much about gender, you attributed your lifelong interest in fluidity and nomadism to being adopted, and you treasured it. You felt you had escaped the fear of someday becoming your parents, a fear you saw ruling the psyches of many of your friends. Your parents didn't have to be disappointments or genetic warnings. They could just be two ordinary people, doing their best. From a very young age—your parents had always been open about the fact that you were adopted—you remember feeling a spreading, inclusive, almost mystical sense of belonging. The fact that anybody could have been your birth mother was an astonishment, but one tinged with exhilaration: rather than being from or for *an* other, you felt you came from the whole world, utterly plural. You were curious enough to track down your birth mother, but after your real mother died, you found yourself unable to answer your birth mother's calls. Even now, years later, the interest you once took in finding her feels clouded by the memory of your mother, and your ongoing grief at losing her. Your longing to see her again. Phyllis.

It's easy enough to say, I'll be the *right* kind of finite or sodomitical mother. I'll let my baby know where the me and the not-me begin and end, and withstand whatever rage ensues. I'll give as much as I've got to give without losing sight of *my own me*. I'll let him know that I'm a person with my own needs and desires, and over time he'll come to respect me for elucidating such boundaries, for feeling real as he comes to know me as real.

But who am I kidding? This book may already be doing wrong. I've heard many people speak with pity about children whose parents wrote about them when they were young. Perhaps the stories of Iggy's origins are not mine alone, and thus not mine alone to tell. Perhaps my temporal proximity to his infancy has led me into a false sense of ownership over his life and body, a sense that is already fading, now that he weighs two pounds more than the heaviest baby ever born, and I no longer have the visceral sense, when beholding him, that he ever could have emerged from me.

Eula Biss *The mother of an adult child sees her work completed and undone at the same time.* If this holds true, I may have to withstand not only rage, but also my undoing. Can one prepare for one's undoing? How has my mother withstood mine? Why do I continue to undo her, when what I want to express above all else is that I love her very much?

What is good is always being destroyed: one of Winnicott's main axioms.

I considered writing Iggy a letter before he was born, but while I talked to him a lot in utero, I stalled out when it came to writing anything down. Writing to him felt akin to giving him a name: an act of love, surely, but also one of irrevocable classification, interpellation. (Perhaps this is why Iggy is named Iggy: if territorialization is inevitable, why not perform it with a little irreverence? "*Iggy:* Not a good choice unless you're planning for a rock star or the class clown," one baby names website warned.) The baby wasn't separate from me, so what use would it be to write to him as if he were off at sea? No need to rehash Linda Hamilton in the final scenes of *The Terminator,* recording an audiotape for her unborn son, the future leader of the human resistance, before she sets off toward Mexico in her beater jeep, storm clouds gathering on the horizon. If you want an original relation to the mother/son dyad, you must turn (however sadly!) away from the seduction of messianic fantasy. And if your baby boy is going to be white, you must become curious about what will happen if you raise him as just another human animal, no more or less worthy than any other.

This is a deflation, but not a dismissal. It is also a new possibility.

When Iggy had the toxin and we lay with him in his hospital crib, I knew—in a flood of fear and panic—what I know now, in our blessed return to the land of health, which is that my time with him has been the happiest time of my life. Its happiness has been of a more palpable and undeniable and unmitigated quality than any I've ever known. For it isn't just moments of happiness, which is all I thought we got. It's a happiness that spreads.

For this reason I am tempted to call it a lasting happiness, but I know I won't take it with me when I go. At best, I hope to impart it to Iggy, to allow him to feel that he created it, which, in many ways, he has.

Babies do not remember being held well—what they remember is the traumatic experience of not being held well enough. Some might read in this a recipe for the classic ungratefulness of children—*after everything I've done for you,* and so on. To me, at the moment anyway, it is a tremendous relief, an incitement to give Iggy *no memory,* save the sense, likely unconscious, of having once been gathered together, made to feel real.

That is what my mother did for me. I'd almost forgotten.

And now, I think I can say—

I want you to know, you were thought of as possible—never as certain, but always as possible—not in any single moment, but over many months, even years, of trying, of waiting, of calling—when, in a love sometimes sure of itself, sometimes shaken by bewilderment and change, but always committed to the charge of ever-deepening understanding—two human animals, one of whom is blessedly neither male nor female, the other of whom is female (more or less), deeply, doggedly, wildly wanted you to be.

After Iggy is released from the hospital post-toxin, we celebrate with one of our living room dance parties, just me and the three Irish guys, so called to honor the otherwise unaddressed genetic link each of them has to Irish stock. We play "Tightrope" by Janelle Monáe over and over again (after years of noise metal, Harry now also keeps abreast of the Top 40, so that he can discuss the finer points of the new Katy Perry, Daft Punk, or Lorde). Iggy's big brother holds him by the armpits and spins him around in a wild circle while we scramble to make sure Iggy's chubby legs don't hit any windows or end tables. As one might expect for brothers seven years apart, they almost always play too rough for my liking. *But he loves it!* his brother says whenever I tell him to take the heavy faux-fur blanket off Iggy's head for a moment, so we can be sure he hasn't smothered. But for the most part, he's right. Iggy loves it. Iggy loves playing with his brother and his brother loves playing with Iggy in ways I could never have dreamt. His brother especially loves dragging Iggy around his schoolyard, bragging about how soft his little brother's head is to mostly preoccupied peers. *Who wants to touch a really soft head?* he yells, as if hawking wares. It stresses me out to watch them play, but it also makes me feel like I've finally done something unequivocally good. That I've finally done my stepson an unequivocal good. *He's mine, all mine,* he says as he scoops Iggy up and runs off with him to another room.

Don't produce and don't reproduce, my friend said. But really there is no such thing as reproduction, only acts of production. No lack, only desiring machines. *Flying anuses, speeding vaginas, there is no castration.* When all the mythologies have been set aside, we can see that, children or no children, *the joke of evolution is that it is a teleology without a point, that we, like all animals, are a project that issues in nothing.*

Andrew Solomon

Deleuze/ Guattari

Phillips/ Bersani

But is there really such a thing as nothing, as nothingness? I don't know. I know we're still here, who knows for how long, ablaze with our care, its ongoing song.

ACKNOWLEDGMENTS

Parts of this book appeared, in different forms, as a talk for *Tendencies* (a series in honor of Eve Kosofsky Sedgwick held at the Graduate Center at the City University of New York, curated by Tim Trace Peterson); as a zine for A. L. Steiner's 2012 *Puppies and Babies* installation (published by Otherwild); in the magazines *jubilat, Tin House,* and *Flaunt;* and in the anthology *After Montaigne* (University of Georgia Press, 2015). This book was supported throughout by a Literature grant from the Creative Capital Foundation, for which I remain grateful.

Special thanks as always to PJ Mark, for his shrewd intelligence and ongoing faith in me: I stand lucky and grateful. Thanks also to Ethan Nosowsky, for his profound editorial wisdom and support, and to Katie Dublinski. For their advice, assistance, and/or inspiration, I also wish to thank Ben Lerner, Eula Biss, Tara Jane ONeil, Wayne Koestenbaum, Steven Marchetti, Brian Blanchfield, Dana Ward, Jmy James Kidd, Macarena Gómez-Barris, Jack Halberstam, Janet Sarbanes, Tara Jepsen, Andrea Fontenot, Amy Sillman, Silas Howard, Peter Gadol, A. L. Steiner, Gretchen Hildebran, Suzanne Snider, Cynthia Nelson, Andrés Gonzalez, Emerson Whitney, Anna Moschovakis, Sarah Manguso, Jessica Kramer, Elena Vogel, Stacey Poston, Melody Moody, Barbara Nelson, Emily Nelson, Craig Tracy, and the Purple Team at the Children's Hospital in Aurora, Colorado.

To my Irish guys: thank you for your daily presence, support, and love. I'm so glad you found me.

In loving memory of those who departed during this book's time: Phyllis DeChant (1938–2010), Eve Kosofsky Sedgwick (1950–2009), Lhasa de Sela (1972–2010), and Maximum Dodge (1993–2012). You are missed.

This book would not exist without Harry Dodge, whose intelligence, foxiness, vision, fortitude, and willingness to be represented have made this project, along with so much else, possible. Thank you for showing me what a nuptial might be—an infinite conversation, an endless becoming.

MAGGIE NELSON is the author of several books of poetry and prose, including *On Freedom: Four Songs of Care and Constraint* (2021), the *New York Times* best seller and National Book Critics Circle Award winner *The Argonauts* (2015), *The Art of Cruelty: A Reckoning* (2011; a *New York Times* Notable Book of the Year), *Bluets* (2009; named by *Bookforum* as one of the top ten best books of the past twenty years), *The Red Parts* (2007; reissued 2016), and *Women, the New York School, and Other True Abstractions* (2007). Her poetry titles include *Something Bright, Then Holes* (2007) and *Jane: A Murder* (2005; finalist for the PEN/Martha Albrand Award for the Art of the Memoir). She has been the recipient of a MacArthur "Genius" Fellowship, a Guggenheim Fellowship, an NEA Fellowship, an Innovative Literature Fellowship from Creative Capital, and an Arts Writers Grant from the Andy Warhol Foundation. She is currently a professor of English at University of Southern California and lives in Los Angeles.

Book design by Rachel Holscher. Composition by Bookmobile Design & Digital Publisher Services, Minneapolis, Minnesota. Manufactured by Versa Press on acid-free, 30 percent post-consumer wastepaper.